I0753379

THE

# LIVING WORD;

OR,

## BIBLE TRUTHS AND LESSONS.

FOR

The Family, the School, and the Church.

Man doth not live by bread only, but by every word that proceedeth out of the mouth of the Lord. — DEUT. viii. 3.

And the Word was made flesh, and dwelt among us. — JOHN i. 14.

BOSTON:
PUBLISHED BY GINN BROTHERS.
1872.

Entered according to Act of Congress, in the year 1872,
BY JAMES C. PARSONS,
in the Office of the Librarian of Congress, at Washington.

University Press: Welch, Bigelow, & Co.,
Cambridge.

# PREFACE.

The aim of this little book is easy to be stated. It is to aid in the presentation of those fundamental religious truths which are nowhere else so practically recognized and so sublimely expressed as in the Semitic Scriptures known as the Holy Bible.

The personal attributes of the Supreme Being, as evidenced in his guiding presence with humanity; the conscious relation of man to him, through the moral sense and spiritual affections, as evidenced in the life of Jesus; and the essential immortality of a life thus hid with Christ in God, as evidenced in its triumph over mortal conditions, — these are the truths which, having in them the quality of inspiration, constitute an inexhaustible source of quickening influence upon the soul. They open forever new depths of spiritual contemplation, and forever new springs of living impulse. They are that deep well of waters springing up into everlasting life.

A serious disadvantage in the reading of the Bible in the family, school, and church arises from the difficulty of making, upon the occasion, a continuous selection of passages setting forth the same general truth or lesson. The effort has here been made to provide such a selection. The method used was to gather from the entire Bible, irrespective of historical sequence, all utterances appealing to the universal religious sentiment or the Christian consciousness, and then to classify them by a natural system, suggested by the obvious meaning of the passages themselves, rather than by any sectarian theory of interpretation.

It is believed that such a book is a demand of the times, and will be eminently useful. Only as it shall prove itself so will it vindicate its claim to existence.

J. C. P.

WALTHAM, May, 1872.

# CONTENTS.

# THE LIVING WORD.

## GOD.

### HIS EXISTENCE.

The place whereon thou standest is holy ground.

There is one God and Father of all, who is above all, and through all, and in you all.

In him we live, and move, and have our being.

Know therefore this day, and consider it in thine heart, that the Lord he is God, in heaven above, and upon the earth beneath; there is none else.

Of him, and through him, and to him are all things; to whom be glory forever.

He that cometh to God must believe that he is, and that he is a rewarder of them that diligently seek him.

## HIS SPIRITUAL, ETERNAL NATURE.

No man hath seen God at any time.

Behold, I go forward, but he is not there; and backward, but I cannot perceive him; on the left hand, where he doth work, but I cannot behold him; he hideth himself on the right hand, that I cannot see him; but he knoweth the way that I take.

Canst thou by searching find out God? Canst thou find out the Almighty unto perfection?

God is great, and we know him not, neither can the number of his years be searched out.

God that made the world and all things therein, seeing that he is Lord of heaven and earth, dwelleth not in temples made with hands; neither is worshipped with men's hands, as though he needed anything, seeing he giveth to all life, breath, and all things; and hath made of one blood all nations of men to dwell on all the face of the earth, and hath determined the times before appointed, and the bounds of their habitation; that they should seek the Lord, if haply they might feel after him, and find him, though he be not far from every one of us. For in him we live, and move, and have our being; as certain also of your own poets have said, "For we are also his offspring." Forasmuch then as we are the offspring of God, we ought not to think that the Godhead is like unto gold or silver or stone, graven by art and man's device.

God is a Spirit, and they that worship him must worship him in spirit and in truth.

Lord, thou hast been our dwelling-place in all generations. Before the mountains were brought forth, or ever thou hadst formed the earth and the world, even from everlasting to everlasting, thou art God.

The King of kings, and Lord of lords, who only hath immortality, dwelling in the light which no man can approach unto, whom no man hath seen nor can see.

## HIS PRESENCE.

Surely the Lord is in this place, and I knew it not. This is none other but the house of God, and this is the gate of heaven.

O Lord, thou hast searched me and known me. Thou knowest my down-sitting and mine up-rising; thou understandest my thought afar off. Thou compassest my path and my lying-down, and art acquainted with all my ways. For there is not a word in my tongue, but lo, O Lord, thou knowest it altogether. Thou hast beset me behind and before, and laid thy hand upon me. Such knowledge is too wonderful for me; it is high; I cannot attain unto it. Whither shall I go from thy Spirit? or whither shall I flee from thy presence? If I ascend up into heaven, thou art there. If I make my bed in the grave, behold thou art there. If I take the wings of the morning, and dwell in the uttermost parts of the sea, even there shall thy hand lead me, and thy right hand shall hold me. If I say, Surely the darkness shall cover me, even the night shall be light about me. Yea, the darkness hideth not from thee; but the night shineth as the day. The darkness and the light are both alike to thee.

Thou, God, seest me.

### HIS POWER.—I. In Nature.

The invisible things of Him from the creation of the world are clearly seen, being understood by the things that are made.

In the beginning, God created the heaven and the earth.

Of old hast thou laid the foundation of the earth, and the heavens are the work of thy hands.

He commanded, and they were created.

By the word of the Lord were the heavens made, and all the host of them by the breath of his mouth. He spake, and it was done; he commanded, and it stood fast.

Whatsoever the Lord pleased, that did he, in heaven, and in earth; in the seas and all deep places.

He sendeth forth his commandment upon earth; his word runneth very swiftly.

And God said, Let there be light; and there was light.

The heavens declare the glory of God, and the firmament showeth his handiwork.

Lift up your eyes on high, and behold who hath created these things, that bringeth out their host by number. He calleth them all by names by the greatness of his might, for that he is strong in power; not one faileth.

He telleth the number of the stars; he calleth them all by their names.

He alone spreadeth out the heavens, and treadeth upon the waves of the sea; he maketh Arcturus, Orion, and Pleiades, and the chambers of the south.

He that maketh the seven stars and Orion, and turneth the shadow of death into the morning, and maketh the day dark with night; that calleth for the waters of the sea, and poureth them out upon the face of the earth; — the Lord is his name.

Lo, he that formeth the mountains, and createth the wind, that maketh the morning darkness, and treadeth upon the high places of the earth, the Lord, the God of hosts, is his name.

The sea is his, and he made it; and his hands formed the dry land.

He bowed the heavens also and came down, and darkness was under his feet.

The Lord hath his way in the whirlwind and in the storm, and the clouds are the dust of his feet.

The voice of the Lord is upon the waters; the God of glory thundereth. The voice of the Lord breaketh the cedars.

God thundereth marvellously with his voice.

He hath made the earth by his power; he hath established the world by his wisdom; when he uttereth his voice, there is a multitude of waters in the heavens, and he causeth the vapors to ascend from the ends of the earth; he maketh lightnings with rain, and bringeth forth the wind out of his treasures.

He covereth the heaven with clouds, he prepareth rain for the earth, he maketh grass to grow upon the mountains.

He saith to the snow, Be thou on the earth; likewise to the small rain, and to the great rain of his strength.

He giveth snow like wool; he scattereth the hoarfrost like ashes. He casteth forth his ice like morsels; who can stand before his cold? He sendeth out his word and melteth them; he causeth his wind to blow, and the waters flow.

Where wast thou, saith the Lord, when I laid the foundations of the earth, when the morning stars sang together, and all the sons of God shouted for joy? Or who shut up the sea with doors, and said, Hitherto shalt thou come, but no farther; and here shall thy proud waves be stayed? Who hath divided a watercourse for the overflowing of waters, to cause it to rain on the earth, where no man is; on the wilderness, where there is no man? Canst thou bind the sweet influences of Pleiades, or loose the bands of Orion? Canst thou bring forth Mazzaroth in his season, or canst thou guide Arcturus with his sons?

Dost thou know the balancings of the clouds, the wondrous works of him who is perfect in knowledge? How thy garments are warm, when he quieteth the earth by the south wind?

In his hand is the soul of every living thing, and the breath of all mankind.

He giveth to the beast his food, and to the young ravens which cry.

For every beast of the forest is his, and the cattle upon a thousand hills.

The young lions roar after their prey, and seek their meat from God. All wait upon thee, that thou mayest give them their meat in due season. That thou givest them, they gather. Thou openest thy hand, they are filled with good. Thou hidest thy face, they are troubled. Thou takest away their breath, they die, and return to their dust. Thou sendest forth thy spirit, they are created, and thou renewest the face of the earth.

Lo, these are parts of his ways; but how little a portion is heard of him? but the thunder of his power who can understand?

God hath spoken once, twice have I heard this, that power belongeth unto God.

The earth is the Lord's and the fulness thereof; the world, and they that dwell therein.

### HIS POWER.—II. AMONG MEN.

Who hath made man's mouth? or who maketh the dumb or deaf, or the seeing or the blind?

He that planted the ear, shall he not hear? He that formed the eye, shall he not see?

He holdeth our soul in life, and suffereth not our feet to be moved.

The Lord killeth and maketh alive; he bringeth down to the grave and bringeth up.

He maketh sore and bindeth up; he woundeth and his hands make whole.

O Lord, I know that the way of man is not in himself; it is not in man that walketh to direct his steps.

A man's heart deviseth his way; but the Lord directeth his steps.

Surely the wrath of man shall praise thee; the remainder of wrath shalt thou restrain.

The Lord bringeth the counsel of the heathen to nought; he maketh the devices of the people of none effect.

Promotion cometh neither from the east, nor from the west, nor from the south. But God is the judge; he putteth down one and setteth up another.

Neither is he that planteth anything, neither he that watereth; but God that giveth the increase.

Hast thou not known, hast thou not heard, that the everlasting God, the Lord, the Creator of the ends of the earth, fainteth not, neither is weary? There is no searching of his understanding. He giveth power to the faint; and to them that have no might, he increaseth strength. Even the youths shall faint and be weary, and the young men shall utterly fall: but they that wait upon the Lord shall renew their strength; they shall mount up with wings as eagles; they shall run and not be weary; and they shall walk and not faint.

It is God that worketh in you both to will and to do of his good pleasure.

All souls are his.

The things which are impossible with men are possible with God.

With God all things are possible.

## HIS WISDOM AND KNOWLEDGE.

O Lord, how manifold are thy works; in wisdom hast thou made them all.

Known unto God are all his works, from the beginning of the world.

One day is with the Lord as a thousand years, and a thousand years as one day.

He hath measured the waters in the hollow of his hand, and meted out heaven with the span, and comprehended the dust of the earth in a measure, and weighed the mountains in scales, and the hills in a balance.

The Lord looketh from heaven; he beholdeth all the sons of men. From the place of his habitation, he looketh upon all the inhabitants of the earth. He fashioneth their hearts alike; he considereth all their works.

His eyes are upon the ways of man, and he seeth all his goings.

The eyes of the Lord are in every place, beholding the evil and the good.

The ways of a man are before the eyes of the Lord, and he pondereth all his goings.

Thine eyes are open upon all the ways of the sons of men, to give to every one according to his ways, and according to the fruit of his doings.

Thou, even thou only, knowest the hearts of all the children of men.

The Lord seeth not as man seeth; for man looketh on the outward appearance, but the Lord looketh on the heart.

The word of God is quick, and powerful, and sharper than any two-edged sword, piercing even to the dividing asunder of soul and spirit; and is a discerner of the thoughts and intents of the heart. Neither is there any creature that is not manifest in his sight; but all things are naked and opened unto the eyes of him with whom we have to do.

O the depth of the riches both of the wisdom and knowledge of God! how unsearchable are his judgments, and his ways past finding out! For who hath known the mind of the Lord? or who hath been his counsellor?

## HIS RIGHTEOUSNESS AND MORAL GOVERNMENT.

There is none good but one, — that is, God.

God is no respecter of persons, but, in every nation, he that feareth him and worketh righteousness is accepted with him.

Good and upright is the Lord.

The word of the Lord is right, and all his works are done in truth. He loveth righteousness and judgment.

Verily there is a reward for the righteous; verily he is a God that judgeth.

The ways of the Lord are right, and the just shall walk in them; but the transgressors shall fall therein.

The way of the wicked is an abomination unto the Lord; but he loveth him that followeth after righteousness.

If I regard iniquity in my heart, the Lord will not hear me.

Thou art of purer eyes than to behold evil, and canst not look on iniquity.

Shall not the Judge of all the earth do right?

The Lord God is merciful and gracious,

long-suffering and abundant in goodness and truth, keeping mercy for thousands, forgiving iniquity and transgression and sin, and who will by no means clear the guilty; visiting the iniquity of the fathers upon the children, and upon the children's children, unto the third and to the fourth generation.

God is not a man, that he should lie; neither the son of man, that he should repent.

The counsel of the Lord standeth forever, the thoughts of his heart to all generations.

There is none holy as the Lord.

Behold God will not cast away a perfect man, neither will he help the evil-doers.

Unto thee, O Lord, belongeth mercy: thou renderest to every man according to his work.

The work of a man shall he render unto him, and cause every man to find according to his ways; yea, surely God will not do wickedly, neither will the Almighty pervert judgment.

He that doeth wrong shall receive for the wrong which he hath done; and there is no respect of persons.

He will render to every man according to his deeds: to them who by patient continuance in well-doing seek for glory and honor and immortality, eternal life; but unto them that are contentious, and do not obey the truth, but obey unrighteousness, indignation and wrath; tribulation and anguish upon every soul of man that doeth evil; but glory, honor, and peace to every man that worketh good; for there is no respect of persons with God.

## HIS LOVE.

The Lord is good to all, and his tender mercies are over all his works.

The earth is full of the goodness of the Lord.

Thou art good and doest good.

Thou preservest man and beast.

Thou openest thy hand and satisfiest the desire of every living thing.

It is of the Lord's mercies that we are not consumed, because his compassions fail not.

He healeth the broken in heart, and bindeth up their wounds.

How excellent is thy loving-kindness, O God! therefore the children of men put their trust under the shadow of thy wings.

The Lord is very pitiful, and of tender mercy.

He forgiveth all thine iniquities; he healeth all thy diseases; he redeemeth thy life from destruction; he crowneth thee with loving-kindness and tender mercies.

Like as a father pitieth his children, so the Lord pitieth them that fear him; for he knoweth our frame; he remembereth that we are dust.

A certain man had two sons: And the younger of them said to his father, "Father, give me the portion of goods that falleth to me." And he divided unto them his living. And not many days after, the younger son gathered all together and took his journey into a far country, and there wasted his substance with riotous living. And when he had spent all, there arose a mighty famine in that land, and he began to be in want. And he went and joined himself to a citizen of that country; and he sent him into his fields to feed swine. And he would fain have filled his belly with the husks that the swine did eat; and no man gave unto him. And when he came to himself, he said, "How many hired servants of my father's have bread enough and to spare, and I perish with hunger. I will arise and go to my father, and will say unto him, 'Father, I have sinned against heaven and before thee, and am no more worthy to be called thy son: make me as one of thy hired servants.'" And he arose, and came to his father. But when he was yet a great way off, his father saw him, and had compassion, and ran, and fell on his neck and kissed him. And the son said unto him, "Father, I have sinned against heaven, and in thy sight, and am no more worthy to be called thy son." But the father said to his servants, "Bring forth the best robe, and put it on him; and put a ring on his hand, and shoes on his feet; and bring hither the fatted calf, and kill it; and let us eat and be merry; for this my son was dead, and is alive again; he was lost, and is found."

Or what man is there of you, whom if his son ask bread, will he give him a stone? or if he ask a fish, will he give him a serpent? If ye, then, being evil, know how to give good gifts unto your children, how much more shall your Father which is in heaven give good things to them that ask him.

Every good gift and every perfect gift is from above, and cometh down from the Father of Lights.

The Lord will not cast off forever; but though he cause grief, yet will he have compassion, according to the multitude of his mercies.

The Lord is not slack concerning his promise, as some men count slackness; but is long-suffering to us-ward, not willing that any should perish, but that all should come to repentance.

It is not the will of your Father which is in heaven that one of these little ones should perish.

The gift of God is eternal life.

For I am persuaded that neither death nor life, nor things present nor things to come, nor height nor depth, shall be able to separate us from the love of God, which is in Christ Jesus our Lord.

For God is Love.

## HIS HELP.

God is our refuge and strength, a very present help in trouble.

My help cometh from the Lord, who made heaven and earth.

Thou art the confidence of all the ends of the earth, and of them that are afar off upon the sea.

The Lord upholdeth all that fall, and raiseth up all those that be bowed down.

We have heard with our ears, O God; our fathers have told us what work thou didst in their days, in the times of old.

The Lord is good, a stronghold in the day of trouble.

Thou, O Lord, art a shield for me.

The Lord is my rock, and my fortress, and my deliverer; my God, my strength, in whom I will trust; my buckler and my high tower.

The Lord is my light and my salvation; whom shall I fear? The Lord is the strength of my life; of whom shall I be afraid?

Though a host should encamp against me, my heart shall not fear.

When my father and my mother forsake me, then the Lord will take me up.

A father of the fatherless, and a judge of the widows, is God in his holy habitation.

The Lord also will be a refuge for the oppressed, a refuge in times of trouble. And they that know thy name will put their trust in thee; for thou, Lord, hast not forsaken them that seek thee.

Though I walk in the midst of trouble, thou wilt revive me.

He shall deliver thee in six troubles; yea, in seven there shall no evil touch thee.

Cast thy burden upon the Lord, and he shall sustain thee.

The eyes of the Lord are upon the righteous, and his ears are open unto their cry. The righteous cry, and the Lord heareth, and delivereth them out of all their troubles.

The Lord redeemeth the soul of his servants; and none of them that trust in him shall be desolate.

The Lord is good unto them that wait for him, to the soul that seeketh him.

In all thy ways acknowledge him, and he shall direct thy paths.

The Lord is nigh unto all them that call upon him, — to all that call upon him in truth.

The Lord is nigh unto them that are of a broken heart, and saveth such as be of a contrite spirit.

He will teach sinners in the way.

The Lord giveth wisdom; out of his mouth cometh knowledge and understanding.

The preparation of the heart in man, and the answer of the tongue, is from the Lord.

Truly my soul waiteth upon God; from him cometh my salvation; he is my defence; I shall not be greatly moved.

Our soul waiteth for the Lord; he is our help and our shield.

Wait on the Lord; be of good courage, and he shall strengthen thy heart; wait, I say, on the Lord.

If God be for us, who can be against us?

## HIS PROMISES.

While the earth remaineth, seed-time and harvest, and cold and heat, and summer and winter, and day and night, shall not cease.

The grass withereth, the flower fadeth; but the word of our God shall stand forever.

Heaven and earth shall pass away, but my words shall not pass away.

The heavens shall vanish away like smoke, and the earth shall wax old like a garment, and they that dwell therein shall die in like manner; but my salvation shall be forever, and my righteousness shall not be abolished.

For as the rain cometh down, and the snow from heaven, and returneth not thither, but watereth the earth, and maketh it bring forth and bud, that it may give seed to the sower and bread to the eater, so shall my word be that goeth forth out of my mouth. It shall not return unto me void, but it shall accomplish that which I please, and it shall prosper in the thing whereto I send it.

I will put my law in their inward parts, and write it in their hearts, and will be their God, and they shall be my people; and they shall teach no more every man his neighbor, and every man his brother, saying, "Know the Lord"; for they shall all know me, from the least of them unto the greatest of them.

And it shall come to pass in the last days,

saith God, I will pour out of my spirit upon all flesh.

And they shall be my people, and I will be their God; and I will give them one heart and one way, that they may fear me forever, for the good of them and of their children after them.

And they shall beat their swords into ploughshares, and their spears into pruning-hooks; nation shall not lift up sword against nation, neither shall they learn war any more.

The earth shall be filled with the knowledge of the glory of the Lord, as the waters cover the sea.

From the rising of the sun, even unto the going down of the same, my name shall be great among the heathen, saith the Lord of hosts.

Behold I bring you good tidings of great joy, which shall be to all people.

Every valley shall be filled, and every mountain and hill shall be brought low; and the crooked shall be made straight, and the rough ways shall be made smooth, and all flesh shall see the salvation of God.

The Spirit itself beareth witness with our

spirit, that we are the children of God; and if children, then heirs; heirs of God, and joint-heirs with Christ.

Now are we the sons of God, and it doth not yet appear what we shall be; but we know that, when he shall appear, we shall be like him; for we shall see him as he is.

The Lord will perfect that which concerneth me.

Other sheep I have, which are not of this fold; them also I must bring, and they shall hear my voice; and there shall be one fold and one shepherd.

As in Adam all die, even so in Christ shall all be made alive.

Then cometh the end, when he shall have delivered up the kingdom to God, even the Father; that God may be all in all.

Eye hath not seen, nor ear heard, neither have entered into the heart of man, the things which God hath prepared for them that love him.

According to his promise, we look for new heavens and a new earth, wherein dwelleth righteousness.

And I saw a new heaven and a new earth,

for the first heaven and the first earth were passed away.

And he that sat upon the throne said, Behold, I make all things new.

And I heard a great voice out of heaven, saying, "Behold the tabernacle of God is with men, and he will dwell with them, and they shall be his people, and God himself shall be with them, and be their God. And God shall wipe away all tears from their eyes; and there shall be no more death, neither sorrow nor crying; neither shall there be any more pain; for the former things are passed away."

---

## MAN.

### HIS SPIRITUAL ORIGIN AND NATURE.

The Lord stretcheth forth the heavens, and layeth the foundation of the earth, and formeth the spirit of man within him.

And the Lord God formed man of the dust of the ground, and breathed into his nostrils the breath of life; and man became a living soul.

It is he that hath made us, and not we ourselves.

In the day that God created man, in the likeness of God made he him.

He created man in his own image.

There is a spirit in man; and the inspiration of the Almighty giveth them understanding.

What is man, that thou art mindful of him? Thou hast made him a little lower than the angels, and hast crowned him with glory and honor. Thou madest him to have dominion over the works of thy hands; thou hast put all things under his feet; all sheep and oxen, yea, and the beasts of the field, the fowl of the air, and the fish of the sea, and whatsoever passeth through the paths of the seas.

I will make a man (saith the Lord) more precious than fine gold; even a man than the golden wedge of Ophir.

Know ye not that ye are the temple of God, and that the spirit of God dwelleth in you?

Know ye not that your body is the temple of the Holy Spirit which is in you, which ye have of God, and ye are not your own? Therefore glorify God in your body, and in your spirit, which are God's.

Behold what manner of love the Father hath bestowed upon us, that we should be called the sons of God.

Now are we the sons of God, and it doth not yet appear what we shall be.

## HIS MORAL SENSE AND ACCOUNTABILITY.

The grace of God that bringeth salvation hath appeared to all men, teaching us that, denying ungodliness and worldly lusts, we should live soberly, righteously, and godly in this present world.

They show the work of the law written in their hearts, their conscience also bearing witness.

For this commandment which I command thee this day, it is not hidden from thee, neither is it far off. It is not in heaven that thou shouldst say, "Who shall go up for us to heaven, and bring it unto us, that we may hear it and do it?" Neither is it beyond the sea, that thou shouldst say, "Who shall go over the sea for us, and bring it unto us, that we may hear it and do it?" But the word is very nigh unto thee, in thy mouth, and in thy heart, that thou mayest do it.

If our heart condemn us, God is greater than our heart, and knoweth all things.

Every one of us shall give account of himself to God.

Unto whomsoever much is given, of him shall be much required.

In every nation he that feareth God, and worketh righteousness, is accepted with him.

If thou doest well, shalt thou not be accepted? And if thou doest not well, sin lieth at the door.

To him that knoweth to do good, and doeth it not, to him it is sin.

The soul that sinneth, *it* shall die. The son shall not bear the iniquity of the father, neither shall the father bear the iniquity of the son; the righteousness of the righteous shall be upon him, and the wickedness of the wicked shall be upon him.

When a righteous man turneth away from his righteousness and committeth iniquity, and dieth in it, — for his iniquity that he hath done, shall he die. Again, when the wicked man turneth away from his wickedness that he hath committed, and doeth that which is lawful and right, he shall save his soul alive.

Let no man deceive you; he that *doeth* righteousness is righteous.

By their fruits ye shall know them. Not every one that saith unto me, "Lord, Lord," shall enter into the kingdom of heaven, but he that doeth the will of my Father which is in heaven.

If thou wilt enter into life, keep the commandments.

Till heaven and earth pass, one jot or one tittle shall in no wise pass from the law till all be fulfilled. Whosoever, therefore, shall break one of these least commandments, and shall teach men so, he shall be called least in the kingdom of heaven; but whosoever shall do and teach them, the same shall be called great in the kingdom of heaven.

Strive to enter in at the strait gate.

For what shall it profit a man, if he shall gain the whole world, and lose his own soul?

Or what shall a man give in exchange for his soul?

God will render to every man according to his deeds.

---

## MORAL AND RELIGIOUS PRECEPTS.

These words which I command thee this day shall be in thine heart, and thou shalt teach them diligently unto thy children, and shalt talk of them when thou sittest in thine house, and when thou walkest by the way, and when thou liest down, and when thou risest up.

My son, hear the instruction of thy father, and forsake not the law of thy mother.

Abhor that which is evil; cleave to that which is good.

If sinners entice thee, consent thou not.

Ponder the path of thy feet, and let all thy ways be established. Turn not to the right hand nor to the left; remove thy foot from evil.

Thou shalt do no murder.

Thou shalt not commit adultery.

Thou shalt not steal.

Thou shalt not bear false witness.

Thou shalt not covet.

Execute true judgment, and show mercy and compassion, every man to his brother; and oppress not the widow, nor the fatherless, the stranger, nor the poor, and let none of you imagine evil against his brother in your heart.

Honor thy father and thy mother.

Remember the Sabbath day to keep it holy.

Thou shalt not take the name of the Lord thy God in vain; for the Lord will not hold him guiltless that taketh his name in vain.

Remember now thy Creator in the days of thy youth, while the evil days come not, nor the years draw nigh when thou shalt say, "I have no pleasure in them."

Seek the Lord, and ye shall live.

Wherewith shall I come before the Lord, and bow myself before the high God?

He hath showed thee, O man, what is good; and what doth the Lord require of thee, but to do justly, and to love mercy, and to walk humbly with thy God?

What doth the Lord thy God require of thee but to fear the Lord thy God, to walk in all his ways, and to love him?

For this is the love of God, that we keep his commandments; and his commandments are not grievous.

Thou shalt love the Lord thy God with all thy heart, and with all thy soul, and with all thy mind, and with all thy strength. This is the first commandment. And the second is like, namely this: Thou shalt love thy neighbor as thyself. There is none other commandment greater than these.

And if there be any other commandment, it is briefly comprehended in this saying, namely, Thou shall love thy neighbor as thyself. Love worketh no ill to his neighbor; therefore love is the fulfilling of the law.

Pure religion and undefiled before God and the Father is this: To visit the fatherless and widows in their affliction, and to keep one's self unspotted from the world.

I beseech you, therefore, by the mercies of God, that ye present your bodies a living sacrifice, holy, acceptable unto God, which is your reasonable service.

Whatsoever things are true, whatsoever things are honest, whatsoever things are just, whatsoever things are pure, whatsoever things are lovely, whatsoever things are of good report, if there be any virtue, and if there be any praise, think on these things.

Let us hear the conclusion of the whole matter: Fear God, and keep his commandments; for this is the whole duty of man. For God shall bring every work into judgment, with every secret thing, whether it be good or whether it be evil.

Be ye therefore perfect, even as your Father which is in heaven is perfect.

Let your light so shine before men, that they may see your good works, and glorify your Father which is in heaven.

---

## SIN AND ITS CONSEQUENCES.

He that doeth wrong shall receive for the wrong which he hath done.

Though hand join in hand, the wicked shall not be unpunished.

There is no darkness nor shadow of death where the workers of iniquity may hide themselves.

Many sorrows shall be to the wicked.

The way of transgressors is hard.

The face of the Lord is against them that do evil.

There is no peace, saith the Lord, unto the wicked.

Evil-doers shall be cut off: their sword shall enter into their own heart.

The ungodly are like the chaff, which the wind driveth away. The way of the ungodly shall perish.

They shall be as the morning-cloud, and as the early dew that passeth away; as the chaff that is driven with the whirlwind out of the floor.

Because I have called and ye refused, I have stretched out my hand and no man regarded; but ye have set at nought all my counsel, and would none of my reproof; therefore shall they eat of the fruit of their own way, and be filled with their own devices.

He that, being often reproved, hardeneth his neck, shall suddenly be destroyed, and that without remedy.

For if we sin wilfully, after that we have received the knowledge of the truth, there remaineth no more sacrifice for sins, but a certain fearful looking-for of judgment, and fiery indignation.

Unto them that are contentious, and do not obey the truth, but obey unrighteousness, tribulation and anguish, upon every soul of man that doeth evil.

As for me, my feet were almost gone, my steps had wellnigh slipped; for I was envious at the foolish, when I saw the prosperity of the wicked: — "They are not in trouble as other men, neither are they plagued like other men; therefore pride compasseth them about as a chain. They set their mouth against the heavens, and their tongue walketh through the earth. And they say, 'How doth God know?' and 'Is there knowledge in the Most High?' Behold, these are the ungodly, who prosper in the world; they increase in riches. Verily, I have cleansed my heart in vain, and washed my hands in innocency." When I thought to know this, it was too painful for me. Until I went into the sanctuary of God; then understood I their end. Surely, thou didst set them in slippery places; thou castedst them down into destruction. How are they brought into desolation as in a moment! They are utterly consumed with terrors.

The wicked flee when no man pursueth.

Woe unto him that buildeth his house by unrighteousness.

Every one that heareth these sayings of mine, and doeth them not, shall be likened unto a foolish man who built his house upon the sand. And the rain descended, and the floods came, and the winds blew, and beat upon that house, and it fell; and great was the fall of it.

Whosoever committeth sin is the servant of sin.

The wages of sin is death.

He that soweth to the flesh, shall of the flesh reap corruption.

To be carnally minded is death.

Sin, when it is finished, bringeth forth death.

If they break my statutes, and keep not my commandments, then will I visit their transgression with the rod, and their iniquity with stripes. Nevertheless, my loving-kindness will I not utterly take from him, nor suffer my faithfulness to fail.

## REPENTANCE AND FORGIVENESS.

God commandeth all men everywhere to repent.

If iniquity be in thine hand, put it far away; then shalt thou lift up thy face without spot; yea, thou shalt be steadfast, and shalt not fear; because thou shalt forget thy misery, and remember it, as waters that pass away; and thine age shall be clearer than the noonday. Thou shalt be secure, because there is hope.

The goodness of God leadeth thee to repentance.

Blessed is he whose transgression is forgiven, whose sin is covered. Blessed is the man to whom the Lord imputeth not iniquity, and in whose spirit there is no guile. I acknowledged my sin unto thee, and mine iniquity have I not hid. I said, I will confess my transgressions unto the Lord, and thou forgavest the iniquity of my sin.

There is joy in the presence of the angels of God over one sinner that repenteth.

The sacrifices of God are a broken spirit; a broken and a contrite heart, O God, thou wilt not despise.

Bring forth, therefore, fruits worthy of repentance.

He that hath two coats, let him impart to him that hath none; and he that hath meat, let him do likewise.

If the wicked will turn from all his sins that he hath committed, and keep all my statutes, and do that which is lawful and right, he shall surely live; he shall not die. All his transgressions that he hath committed, they shall not be mentioned unto him; in his righteousness that he hath done, he shall live.

Godly sorrow worketh repentance to salvation, not to be repented of.

I will hear what God the Lord will speak; for he will speak peace unto his people and to his saints; but let them not turn again to folly.

Go, and sin no more.

---

## OBEDIENCE AND ITS CONSEQUENCES.

### I. WELFARE.

TRUST in the Lord, and do good; so shalt thou dwell in the land, and verily thou shalt be fed.

There is no want to them that fear him. The young lions do lack, and suffer hunger; but they that seek the Lord shall not want any good thing.

Delight thyself also in the Lord, and he shall give thee the desires of thine heart. Commit thy way unto the Lord; trust also in him, and he shall bring it to pass. He shall bring forth thy righteousness as the light, and thy judgment as the noonday.

The meek shall inherit the earth.

A little that a righteous man hath, is better than the riches of many wicked.

Though a sinner do evil a hundred times, and his days be prolonged, yet surely I know that it shall be well with them that fear God.

Seek first the kingdom of God and his righteousness, and all these things shall be added unto you.

### II. SECURITY.

Lord, who shall abide in thy tabernacle? who shall dwell in thy holy hill? He that walketh uprightly, and worketh righteousness, and speaketh the truth in his heart. He that doeth these things shall never be moved.

Blessed is the man that feareth the Lord,—that delighteth greatly in his commandments. Surely he shall not be moved forever. He shall not be afraid of evil tidings. His heart is fixed, trusting in the Lord. His heart is established; he shall not be afraid.

He that trusteth in the Lord, mercy shall compass him about.

The angel of the Lord encampeth round about them that fear him, and delivereth them.

Because thou hast made the Lord, even the Most High, thy habitation, he shall give his angels charge over thee, to keep thee in all thy ways.

Whosoever heareth these sayings of mine, and doeth them, I will liken him unto a wise man, who built his house upon a rock. And the rain descended, and the floods came, and the winds blew, and beat upon that house, and it fell not; for it was founded upon a rock.

They that trust in the Lord shall be as Mount Zion, which cannot be removed, but abideth forever.

## III. WISDOM.

Unto the upright there ariseth light in the darkness.

Light is sown for the righteous, and gladness for the upright in heart.

The fear of the Lord is the beginning of wisdom. A good understanding have all they that do his commandments.

The secret of the Lord is with them that fear him.

What man is he that feareth the Lord? Him shall he teach in the way that he shall choose.

I have more understanding than all my teachers, for thy testimonies are my meditation. I understand more than the ancients, because I keep thy precepts.

They that seek the Lord understand all things.

If any man will do his will, he shall know of the doctrine.

Ye shall know the truth, and the truth shall make you free.

### IV. PEACE.

When he giveth quietness, who then can make trouble?

Thou wilt keep him in perfect peace whose mind is stayed on thee.

When a man's ways please the Lord, he

maketh even his enemies to be at peace with him.

To be spiritually minded is life and peace.

Blessed are they which do hunger and thirst after righteousness; for they shall be filled.

Mark the perfect man, and behold the upright; for the end of that man is peace.

## V. GOD'S FAVOR AND ETERNAL LIFE.

In every nation, he that feareth God and worketh righteousness is accepted with him.

Blessed is the man that walketh not in the counsel of the ungodly, nor standeth in the way of sinners; but his delight is in the law of the Lord, and in his law doth he meditate day and night. He shall be like a tree planted by the rivers of water, that bringeth forth its fruit in its season. His leaf also shall not wither, and whatsoever he doeth shall prosper.

The steps of a good man are ordered by the Lord, and he delighteth in his way. Though he fall, he shall not be utterly cast down, for the Lord upholdeth him with his hand.

Thou, Lord, wilt bless the righteous; with favor wilt thou compass him, as with a shield.

Who shall ascend into the hill of the Lord? Or who shall stand in his holy place? He that hath clean hands and a pure heart. He shall receive the blessing from the Lord, and righteousness from the God of his salvation.

All the paths of the Lord are mercy and truth unto such as keep his covenant and his testimonies.

O how great is thy goodness which thou hast laid up for them that fear thee!

O, taste and see that the Lord is good! Blessed is the man that trusteth in him.

Blessed is the man whom thou choosest, and causest to approach unto thee, that he may dwell in thy courts.

In thy presence is fulness of joy; at thy right hand there are pleasures forevermore.

Blessed are the pure in heart, for they shall see God.

All things work together for good to them that love God.

Whatsoever a man soweth, that shall he also reap. He that soweth to the Spirit, shall of the Spirit reap life everlasting.

God will render to every man according to his deeds; to them who by patient continuance in well-doing seek for glory and honor and immortality, eternal life.

Godliness is profitable unto all things; having promise of the life that now is, and of that which is to come.

---

## SEEKING THE SPIRIT.

SEEK ye the Lord while he may be found, call ye upon him while he is near. Let the wicked forsake his way, and the unrighteous man his thoughts; and let him return unto the Lord, and he will have mercy upon him; and to our God, for he will abundantly pardon.

When thou saidst, "Seek ye my face," my heart said unto thee, "Thy face, Lord, will I seek."

Lord, what wilt thou have me to do?

And it came to pass at that time, when Eli was laid down in his place, and his eyes began to wax dim, that he could not see, and ere the lamp of God went out in the temple of the Lord, where the ark of God was, and Samuel was laid down to sleep, that the Lord called Samuel; and he answered, "Here am I." And he ran unto Eli, and said, "Here am I, for thou calledst me." And he said, "I called not; lie down again." And he went and lay down. And the Lord called yet again, "Samuel." And Samuel arose and went to Eli, and said, "Here am I; for thou didst call me." And he answered, "I called not, my son; lie down again." Now Samuel did not yet know the Lord, neither was the word of the Lord yet revealed unto him. And the Lord called Samuel again the third time. And he arose and went to Eli, and said, "Here am I, for thou didst call me." And Eli perceived that the Lord had called the child. Therefore Eli said unto Samuel, "Go, lie down, and it shall be, if he call thee, that thou shalt say, 'Speak, Lord; for thy servant heareth.'" So Samuel went and lay down in his place. And the Lord came and stood and called as at other times, "Samuel, Samuel." Then Samuel answered, "Speak, for thy servant heareth."

Stand in awe, and sin not; commune with your own heart upon your bed, and be still.

Behold, I stand at the door and knock; if any man hear my voice, and open the door, I will come in to him.

If a man love me, he will keep my words; and my Father will love him, and we will come unto him, and make our abode with him.

Quench not the Spirit.

Ask, and it shall be given you; seek, and ye shall find; knock, and it shall be opened unto you.

Ye shall seek me and find me, when ye shall search for me with all your heart.

If ye, being evil, know how to give good gifts unto your children, how much more shall your heavenly Father give the Holy Spirit to them that ask him.

As many as are led by the Spirit of God, they are the sons of God.

The fruit of the Spirit is love, joy, peace, long-suffering, gentleness, goodness, faith, meekness, temperance.

The fruit of the Spirit is in all goodness and righteousness and truth.

---

## PRAYER.

He that cometh to God must believe that he is, and that he is a rewarder of them that diligently seek him.

When thou prayest, enter into thy closet, and when thou hast shut thy door, pray to thy Father who is in secret; and thy Father who seeth in secret shall reward thee openly. But when ye pray, use not vain repetitions, as the heathen do: for they think that they shall be heard for their much speaking. Be not ye therefore like unto them, for your Father knoweth what things ye have need of before ye ask him. After this manner, therefore, pray ye: —

Our Father who art in heaven, hallowed be thy name. Thy kingdom come. Thy will be done, in earth as it is in heaven. Give us this day our daily bread. And forgive us our debts, as we forgive our debtors. And lead us not into temptation, but deliver us from evil. For thine is the kingdom, and the power, and the glory, forever. Amen.

For, if ye forgive men their trespasses, your heavenly Father will also forgive you.

Therefore, if thou bring thy gift to the altar, and there rememberest that thy brother hath aught against thee, leave there thy gift before the altar, and go thy way: first be reconciled to thy brother, and then come and offer thy gift.

If any man be a worshipper of God, and doeth his will, him God heareth.

The eyes of the Lord are over the righteous, and his ears are open unto their prayers.

If any of you lack wisdom, let him ask of God, who giveth to all men liberally, and upbraideth not; and it shall be given him. But let him ask in faith, nothing wavering.

And all things whatsoever ye shall ask in prayer, believing, ye shall receive.

Ask, and it shall be given you; seek, and ye shall find; knock, and it shall be opened unto you. For every one that asketh, receiveth; and he that seeketh, findeth; and to him that knocketh, it shall be opened. If ye, being evil, know how to give good gifts unto your children, how much more shall your heavenly Father give the Holy Spirit to them that ask him.

And when they had prayed, they were all filled with the Holy Spirit, and they spake the word of God with boldness.

Continue in prayer, and watch in the same, with thanksgiving.

Draw nigh to God, and he will draw nigh to you.

Pray without ceasing.

Men ought always to pray, and not to faint.

---

## CONQUERING TEMPTATION.

My son, if sinners entice thee, consent thou not.

Watch and pray, lest ye enter into temptation.

Let him that thinketh he standeth, take heed lest he fall.

Enter ye in at the strait gate.

Let no man say, when he is tempted, I am tempted of God; for God cannot be tempted with evil, neither tempteth he any man; but every man is tempted when he is drawn away of his own lust, and enticed.

God will not suffer you to be tempted above that ye are able; but will, with the temptation, also make a way to escape, that ye may be able to bear it.

He that hath no rule over his own spirit is like a city that is broken down, and without walls.

He that ruleth his spirit is better than he that taketh a city.

Blessed is the man that endureth temptation; for when he is tried, he shall receive the crown of life which the Lord hath promised to them that love him.

Who can find a virtuous woman? for her price is far above rubies. Favor is deceitful, and beauty is vain, but a woman that feareth the Lord, she shall be praised.

Be thou faithful unto death, and I will give thee a crown of life.

To him that overcometh will I give to eat of the tree of life, which is in the midst of the paradise of God.

He that overcometh shall inherit all things; and I will be his God, and he shall be my son.

---

## TRUTH AND HONESTY.

We can do nothing against the truth, but for the truth.

If a man strive for masteries, yet is he not crowned except he strive lawfully.

Thou shalt not bear false witness.

Wherefore, putting away lying, speak every man truth with his neighbor.

Woe to him that buildeth a town with blood, and establisheth a city by iniquity!

Divers weights and divers measures, both of them alike are abomination to the Lord.

Shall I count them pure with the wicked balances and with the bag of deceitful weights?

Prove all things; hold fast that which is good.

---

## PURITY OF THOUGHT AND SPEECH.

Abstain from all appearance of evil.

Keep thyself pure.

Flee also youthful lusts, but follow righteousness, faith, charity, peace, with them that call on the Lord out of a pure heart.

Unto the pure all things are pure; but unto them that are defiled and unbelieving is nothing pure; but even their mind and conscience is defiled.

Let no corrupt communication proceed out of your mouth.

Let your conversation be as becometh the gospel of Christ.

Let your speech be always with grace.

Be not rash with thy mouth, and let not thy heart be hasty to utter anything before God. For God is in heaven, and thou upon earth; therefore let thy words be few.

Wherefore let every man be swift to hear, slow to speak, slow to wrath.

If any man among you seem to be religious, and bridleth not his tongue, but deceiveth his own heart, this man's religion is vain.

He that will love life, and see good days, let him refrain his tongue from evil, and his lips, that they speak no guile.

The tongue is a little member, and boasteth great things. Behold how great a matter a little fire kindleth! Who is a wise man and endued with knowledge among you? Let him show out of a good conversation his works with meekness of wisdom.

I say unto you, that every idle word that men shall speak, they shall give account thereof in the day of judgment. For by thy words thou shalt be justified, and by thy words thou shalt be condemned.

Speak not evil one of another.

Swear not at all; neither by heaven, for it is God's throne; nor by the earth, for it is his footstool; neither shalt thou swear by thy head, because thou canst not make one hair white or black. But let your communication be "Yea, yea"; "Nay, nay": for whatsoever is more than these cometh of evil.

---

## TEMPERANCE.

Be not drunk with wine; wherein is excess.

Wine is a mocker; strong drink is raging; and whosoever is deceived thereby is not wise.

They have erred through wine, and through strong drink are out of the way; they err in vision; they stumble in judgment.

Who hath woe? who hath sorrow? who hath contentions? who hath babbling? who hath wounds without cause? who hath redness of eyes? They that tarry long at the wine; they that go to seek mixed wine. Look not thou upon the wine when it is red, when it giveth its color in the cup, when it moveth itself aright. At the last it biteth like a serpent, and stingeth like an adder. Thine eyes shall behold strange women, and thine heart shall utter perverse things; yea, thou shalt be as he that lieth down in the midst of the sea, or as he that lieth upon the top of a mast. "They have stricken me," shalt thou say, "and I was not sick; they have beaten me, and I felt it not; when shall I awake? I will seek it yet again."

Woe unto him that giveth his neighbor drink, that puttest thy bottle to him, and makest him drunken also!

Be not amongst wine-bibbers.

---

## THE STRANGE WOMAN.

DISCRETION shall preserve thee; understanding shall keep thee; to deliver thee from the strange woman, even from the stranger which flattereth with her words. Who forsaketh the guide of her youth, and forgetteth the covenant of her God. For her house inclineth unto death, and her paths unto the dead.

Let not thine heart decline to her ways; go not astray in her paths; for she hath cast down many wounded; yea, many strong men have been slain by her. Her house is the way to hell, going down to the chambers of death.

Remove thy way far from her, and come not nigh the door of her house; lest thou give thine honor unto others, and thy years unto the cruel; and thou mourn at the last, when thy flesh and thy body are consumed; and say, How have I hated instruction, and my heart despised reproof!

His own iniquities shall take the wicked himself, and he shall be holden with the cords of his sins.

---

## A VIRTUOUS WOMAN.

WHO can find a virtuous woman? for her price is far above rubies. The heart of her husband doth safely trust in her. She will do him good, and not evil, all the days of her life.

She seeketh wool and flax, and worketh willingly with her hands. She girdeth her loins with strength, and strengtheneth her arms. She looketh well to the ways of her household, and eateth not the bread of idleness.

She stretcheth out her hand to the poor; yea, she reacheth forth her hands to the needy. She openeth her mouth with wisdom, and in her tongue is the law of kindness.

Strength and honor are her clothing, and she shall rejoice in time to come. Her children arise up and call her blessed; her husband, also, and he praiseth her.

Many daughters have done virtuously, but thou excellest them all. Favor is deceitful, and beauty is vain; but a woman that feareth the Lord, she shall be praised. Give her of the fruit of her hands, and let her own works praise her in the gates.

---

## PARENTS AND CHILDREN.

Take heed that ye despise not one of these little ones; for I say unto you that in heaven their angels do always behold the face of my Father which is in heaven.

It is not the will of your Father which is in

heaven that one of these little ones should perish.

Fathers, provoke not your children to anger, lest they be discouraged.

But bring them up in the nurture and admonition of the Lord.

Train up a child in the way he should go, and when he is old he will not depart from it.

Children, obey your parents in the Lord; for this is right.

Obey your parents in all things; for this is well pleasing unto the Lord.

Honor thy father and mother.

Even a child is known by his doings, whether his work be pure, and whether it be right.

---

## WORK.

WHATSOEVER thy hand findeth to do, do it with thy might.

Whatsoever ye do, do it heartily, as to the Lord, and not unto men.

Every tree is known by its own fruit.

Herein is my Father glorified, that ye bear much fruit.

I went by the field of the slothful, and by the vineyard of the man void of understanding. And lo, it was all grown over with thorns, and nettles had covered the face thereof, and the stone wall thereof was broken down. Then I saw and considered it well; I looked upon it and received instruction. Yet a little sleep, a little slumber, a little folding of the hands to sleep. So shall thy poverty come as one that travelleth, and thy want as an armed man.

Know ye not that they which run in a race, all run, but one receiveth the prize? So run that ye may obtain.

The night cometh when no man can work.

Walk while ye have the light, lest darkness come upon you.

Therefore let us not sleep, as do others; but let us watch and be sober.

---

## FAITH, COURAGE, AND ZEAL.

FAITH is the substance of things hoped for, the evidence of things not seen.

In God have I put my trust; I will not fear what flesh can do unto me.

Fear not (saith God), I am thy shield and thy exceeding great reward.

Be not afraid of sudden fear, for the Lord shall be thy confidence.

Be strong and of a good courage; for the Lord thy God, he it is that doth go with thee.

Be thou strong, and show thyself a man.

Be strong in the Lord, and in the power of his might.

Quit you like men.

By faith Moses chose rather to suffer affliction with the people of God, than to enjoy the pleasures of sin for a season.

Whatsoever ye do, do it heartily, as to the Lord, and not unto men.

It is good to be zealously affected always in a good thing.

Whether it be right in the sight of God to hearken unto you more than unto God, judge ye.

We ought to obey God rather than men.

If God be for us, who can be against us?

All things are possible to him that believeth.

Wherefore, seeing we also are compassed about with so great a cloud of witnesses, let us lay aside every weight, and the sin which doth so easily beset us, and let us run with patience the race that is set before us.

Forgetting those things which are behind, and reaching forth unto those things which are before, press toward the mark for the prize of the high calling of God in Christ Jesus.

Wherefore take unto you the whole armor of God, that ye may be able to withstand in the evil day, and, having done all, to stand. Stand, therefore, having your loins girt about with truth, and having on the breastplate of righteousness, and your feet shod with the preparation of the gospel of peace; above all, taking the shield of faith, wherewith ye shall be able to quench all the fiery darts of the wicked.

Whatsoever is born of God overcometh the world; and this is the victory that overcometh the world, even our faith.

---

## TRUST AND CONTENT.

I HAVE learned in whatsoever state I am therewith to be content.

Take no thought for the morrow; for the

morrow shall take thought for the things of itself.

Behold the fowls of the air, for they sow not, neither do they reap, nor gather into barns; yet your heavenly Father feedeth them. Are ye not much better than they?

Are not five sparrows sold for two farthings, and not one of them is forgotten before God? But even the very hairs of your head are all numbered. Fear not, therefore; ye are of more value than many sparrows.

And why take ye thought for raiment? Consider the lilies of the field, how they grow; they toil not, neither do they spin; and yet I say unto you that even Solomon, in all his glory, was not arrayed like one of these. Wherefore, if God so clothe the grass of the field, which to-day is, and to-morrow is cast into the oven, shall he not much more clothe you, O ye of little faith?

Having food and raiment, let us be there-with content.

Thou art careful and troubled about many things; but one thing is needful.

Be careful for nothing; but in everything by prayer and supplication, with thanksgiving, let your request be made known unto God.

Although the fig-tree shall not blossom, neither shall fruit be in the vines, the labor of the olive shall fail, and the fields shall yield no meat, the flock shall be cut off from the fold, and there shall be no herd in the stalls; yet I will rejoice in the Lord, I will joy in the God of my salvation.

It is good that a man should both hope and quietly wait for the salvation of the Lord.

The Lord taketh pleasure in those that hope in his mercy.

For God hath not given us the spirit of fear; but of power, and of love, and of a sound mind.

Commit thy way unto the Lord; trust also in him, and he shall bring it to pass.

Blessed is the man that trusteth in the Lord.

Trust in him at all times.

---

## WISDOM: HUMAN AND DIVINE.

Where shall wisdom be found, and where is the place of understanding? It cannot be gotten for gold neither shall silver be weighed for the price thereof. No mention shall be made of coral, or of pearls; for the price of wisdom is above rubies. Behold, the fear of the Lord, that is wisdom; and to depart from evil is understanding.

Wisdom is more precious than rubies, and all the things thou canst desire are not to be compared unto her. Length of days is in her right hand, and in her left hand riches and honor. Her ways are ways of pleasantness, and all her paths are peace.

My son, hear the instruction of thy father, and forsake not the law of thy mother; for they shall be an ornament of grace unto thy head, and chains about thy neck.

Then shalt thou walk in thy way safely, and thy foot shall not stumble. When thou liest down, thou shalt not be afraid. Yea, thou shalt lie down, and thy sleep shall be sweet.

Enter not into the path of the wicked, and go not in the way of evil men. Avoid it, pass not by it, turn from it, and pass away. But the path of the just is as the shining light, that shineth more and more unto the perfect day.

Keep thy heart with all diligence, for out of it are the issues of life. Let thine eyes look right on, and let thine eyelids look straight before thee. Ponder the path of thy feet, and let all thy ways be established. Turn not to the right hand nor to the left; remove thy foot from evil.

Whoso keepeth the law is a wise son; but he that is a companion of riotous men shameth his father.

The simple believeth every word; but the prudent man looketh well to his going.

Better is little with the fear of the Lord, than great treasure and trouble therewith. Better is a dinner of herbs where love is, than a stalled ox and hatred therewith.

A good name is rather to be chosen than great riches, and loving favor rather than silver and gold.

Train up a child in the way he should go; and when he is old he will not depart from it.

A wise son maketh a glad father; but a foolish man despiseth his mother.

Boast not thyself of to-morrow, for thou knowest not what a day may bring forth. Let another man praise thee, and not thine own mouth; a stranger, and not thine own lips.

Trust in the Lord with all thine heart, and lean not unto thine own understanding.

Let not the wise man glory in his wisdom, neither let the mighty man glory in his might; let not the rich man glory in his riches; but let him that glorieth glory in this, that he understandeth and knoweth me, that I am the Lord, who exercise loving-kindness, judgment, and righteousness in the earth.

Let your light so shine before men, that they may see your good works and glorify your Father which is in heaven.

Even a child is known by his doings, whether his work be pure, and whether it be right.

Walk as children of light.

---

## HUMILITY.

Blessed are the meek; for they shall inherit the earth.

Blessed are the poor in spirit; for theirs is the kingdom of heaven.

God resisteth the proud, but giveth grace unto the humble.

Whosoever exalteth himself shall be abased, and he that humbleth himself shall be exalted.

Charge them that are rich in this world, that they be not high-minded.

When thou doest thine alms, do not sound a trumpet before thee.

Let nothing be done through strife or vainglory; but in lowliness of mind let each esteem other better than themselves. Look not every man on his own things, but every man also on the things of others.

For I say, through the grace given unto me, to every man that is among you, not to think of himself more highly than he ought to think.

He that glorieth, let him glory in the Lord; for not he that commendeth himself is approved, but whom the Lord commendeth.

Whosoever shall not receive the kingdom of God as a little child, he shall not enter therein.

I thank thee, O Father, [said Jesus,] because thou hast hid these things from the wise and prudent, and hast revealed them unto babes.

Walk worthy of the vocation wherewith ye are called, with all lowliness and meekness, with long-suffering, forbearing one another in love.

God be merciful to me a sinner!

---

## PUTTING AWAY WRATH.

He that is slow to anger is better than the mighty.

He that is soon angry dealeth foolishly.

A wrathful man stirreth up strife; but he that is slow to anger appeaseth strife.

A soft answer turneth away wrath; but grievous words stir up anger.

The wrath of man worketh not the righteousness of God.

Let all bitterness and wrath and anger and clamor and evil-speaking be put away from you, with all malice.

Be at peace among yourselves. See that none render evil for evil unto any man; but ever follow that which is good, both among yourselves, and to all men.

Follow peace with all men, and holiness, without which no man shall see the Lord.

Let not the sun go down upon your wrath.

Blessed are the peacemakers, for they shall be called the children of God.

Be not overcome of evil, but overcome evil with good.

Behold how good and how pleasant it is for brethren to dwell together in unity.

Dearly beloved, avenge not yourselves, but rather give place unto wrath; for it is written, Vengeance is mine; I will repay, saith the Lord.

The servant of the Lord must not strive; but be gentle unto all men, patient, in meekness instructing those that oppose themselves.

In malice, be ye children; but in understanding, be men.

Do all things without murmurings and disputings; that ye may be blameless and harmless, the sons of God, without rebuke.

Let us therefore follow after the things which make for peace, and things wherewith one may edify another.

## PATIENCE.

He that shall endure unto the end, the same shall be saved.

No man, having put his hand to the plough, and looking back, is fit for the kingdom of God.

Let us not be weary in well doing; for in due season we shall reap, if we faint not.

Let patience have her perfect work.

In your patience possess ye your souls.

Let your moderation be known unto all men.

Behold the husbandman waiteth for the precious fruit of the earth, and hath long patience for it, until he receive the early and latter rain; be ye also patient.

Therefore, be ye steadfast, unmovable, abounding in the work of the Lord, forasmuch as ye know that your labor is not in vain in the Lord.

This is thankworthy, if a man for conscience toward God endure grief, suffering wrongfully. For what glory is it, if, when ye be buffeted for your faults, ye shall take it patiently? But if, when ye do well, and suffer for it, ye shall take it patiently, this is acceptable with God.

## CHARITY AND FORGIVENESS.

Blessed are the merciful; for they shall obtain mercy.

Judge not, that ye be not judged.

And why beholdest thou the mote that is in thy brother's eye, but perceivest not the beam that is in thine own eye?

All things whatsoever ye would that men should do to you, do ye even so to them; for this is the law and the prophets.

Brethren, if a man be overtaken in a fault, ye which are spiritual, restore such a one in the spirit of meekness; considering thyself, lest thou also be tempted.

If thy brother shall trespass against thee, go and tell him his fault between thee and him alone; if he shall hear thee, thou hast gained thy brother.

If thy brother trespass against thee, rebuke him; and if he repent, forgive him.

How oft shall my brother sin against me, and I forgive him? till seven times? — I say not unto thee, until seven times, but until seventy times seven.

Put on, therefore, kindness, humbleness of

mind, meekness, long-suffering, forbearing one another, and forgiving one another, if any man have a quarrel against any.

Above all these things, put on charity, which is the bond of perfectness.

Charity suffereth long and is kind ; charity envieth not; charity vaunteth not itself, is not puffed up, seeketh not her own, is not easily provoked, thinketh no evil; rejoiceth not in iniquity, but rejoiceth in the truth ; beareth all things, believeth all things, hopeth all things, endureth all things. Charity never faileth ; but whether there be prophecies, they shall fail ; whether there be tongues, they shall cease ; whether there be knowledge, it shall vanish away.

For we know in part, and we prophesy in part. But when that which is perfect is come, then that which is in part shall be done away.

When I was a child, I spake as a child, I understood as a child, I thought as a child ; but when I became a man I put away childish things. For now we see through a glass darkly, but then face to face. Now I know in part, but then shall I know even as also I am known.

And now abideth faith, hope, charity, these three; but the greatest of these is charity.

---

## DOING GOOD TO OTHERS.

THOU shalt not harden thine heart, nor shut thine hand from thy poor brother; but thou shalt open thine hand wide unto him, and shalt surely lend him sufficient for his need, in that which he wanteth.

Withhold not good from them to whom it is due, when it is in the power of thy hand to do it. Say not unto thy neighbor, "Go, and come again, and to-morrow I will give," when thou hast it by thee.

If a brother or sister be naked, and destitute of daily food, and one of you say unto them, "Depart in peace; be ye warmed and filled," notwithstanding ye give them not those things which are needful to the body, what doth it profit?

Do good, and lend, hoping for nothing again.

He that giveth unto the poor shall not lack.

Freely ye have received, freely give.

Remember the words of the Lord Jesus, how he said, "It is more blessed to give than to receive."

The Son of man came not to be ministered unto, but to minister.

He that soweth sparingly shall reap also sparingly; and he that soweth bountifully shall reap also bountifully. Every man according as he purposeth in his heart, so let him give; not grudgingly, or of necessity; for God loveth a cheerful giver.

Rejoice with them that do rejoice, and weep with them that weep.

Be not forgetful to entertain strangers; remember them that are in bonds, as bound with them; and them which suffer adversity, as being yourselves also in the body.

If thine enemy be hungry, give him bread to eat; and if he be thirsty, give him water to drink.

As ye would that men should do to you, do ye also to them.

## LOVE.

Ye have heard that it hath been said, Thou shalt love thy neighbor, and hate thine enemy; but I say unto you, Love your enemies, bless them that curse you, do good to them that hate you, and pray for them which despitefully use you and persecute you; that ye may be the children of your Father which is in heaven. For he maketh his sun to rise on the evil and on the good, and sendeth rain on the just and on the unjust.

He that loveth not his brother, whom he hath seen, how can he love God, whom he hath not seen?

Therefore, if thou bring thy gift to the altar, and there rememberest that thy brother hath aught against thee, leave there thy gift before the altar, and go thy way; first be reconciled to thy brother, and then come and offer thy gift.

He that loveth his brother abideth in the light.

But he that hateth his brother is in darkness, and walketh in darkness, and knoweth not whither he goeth, because that darkness hath blinded his eyes.

Whosoever doeth not righteousness is not of God, neither he that loveth not his brother.

He that dwelleth in love, dwelleth in God, and God in him.

My little children, let us not love in word, neither in tongue, but in deed and in truth.

Love worketh no ill to his neighbor, therefore love is the fulfilling of the law.

Be kindly affectioned one to another with brotherly love; in honor preferring one another.

Love as brethren; be pitiful; be courteous; not rendering evil for evil, or railing for railing, but contrariwise blessing.

Beloved, let us love one another. For love is of God; and every one that loveth is born of God and knoweth God. God is love, and he that dwelleth in love dwelleth in God, and God in him. There is no fear in love; but perfect love casteth out fear.

This commandment have we from him, That he who loveth God love his brother also.

## HUMAN BROTHERHOOD.

God hath made of one blood all nations of men, to dwell on all the face of the earth.

For we are members one of another.

As we have many members in one body, and all members have not the same office, so we, being many, are one body in Christ, and every one members one of another.

The eye cannot say unto the hand, " I have no need of thee" ; nor again, the head to the feet, " I have no need of you." Whether one member suffer, all the members suffer with it; or one member be honored, all the members rejoice with it.

Look not every man on his own things, but every man also on the things of others.

Bear ye one another's burdens, and so fulfil the law of Christ.

---

## SPIRITUAL LIFE.

Blessed are they that do hunger and thirst after righteousness.

Ho, every one that thirsteth, come ye to the

waters; and he that hath no money; come ye, buy and eat.

The water that I shall give him shall be in him a well of water springing up into everlasting life.

Wherefore do ye spend money for that which is not bread, and your labor for that which satisfieth not?

Labor not for the meat that perisheth, but for that meat which endureth to everlasting life.

Man shall not live by bread alone, but by every word that proceedeth out of the mouth of God.

The kingdom of God is not meat and drink, but righteousness, peace, and joy, in the Holy Spirit.

A man's life consisteth not in the abundance of the things which he possesseth.

If riches increase, set not your heart upon them.

A little that a righteous man hath, is better than the riches of many wicked.

Lay not up for yourselves treasures upon earth, where moth and rust doth corrupt, and where thieves break through and steal; but lay up for yourselves treasures in heaven, where neither moth nor rust doth corrupt, and where thieves do not break through nor steal; for where your treasure is, there will your heart be also.

For we brought nothing into this world, and it is certain we can carry nothing out.

It is the spirit that quickeneth; the flesh profiteth nothing.

The kingdom of God is within you.

To be spiritually minded is life and peace.

Howbeit, that was not first which is spiritual, but that which is natural; and afterward that which is spiritual.

The natural man receiveth not the things of the Spirit of God, for they are foolishness unto him; neither can he know them, because they are spiritually discerned.

I find a law that when I would do good, evil is present with me; for I delight in the law of God after the inward man, but I see another law in my members, warring against the law of my mind. O wretched man that I am! who shall deliver me from the body of this death? I thank God, through Jesus Christ our Lord. For the law of the Spirit of life in Christ Jesus hath made me free from the law of sin and death.

Where the spirit of the Lord is, there is liberty.

Hereby know we that we dwell in him, and he in us, because he hath given us of his Spirit.

His divine power hath given unto us all things that pertain unto life and godliness, through the knowledge of him that hath called us to glory and virtue; whereby are given unto us exceeding great and precious promises, that by these ye might be partakers of the divine nature, having escaped the corruption that is in the world through lust.

Be ye therefore followers of God, as dear children, and walk in love.

The wisdom that is from above is first pure, then peaceable, gentle, and easy to be entreated, full of mercy and good fruits, without partiality and without hypocrisy.

Be not conformed to this world; but be ye transformed, by the renewing of your mind, that ye may prove what is that good and acceptable and perfect will of God.

Rejoicing in hope; patient in tribulation; continuing instant in prayer.

Add to your faith, virtue; and to virtue,

knowledge; and to knowledge, temperance; and to temperance, patience; and to patience, godliness; and to godliness, brotherly kindness; and to brotherly kindness, charity.

The end of the commandment is charity, out of a pure heart, and of a good conscience, and of faith unfeigned.

Follow after righteousness, godliness, faith, love, patience, meekness. Fight the good fight of faith; lay hold on eternal life.

The world passeth away, and the lust thereof, but he that doeth the will of God abideth forever.

Godliness is profitable unto all things, having promise of the life that now is, and of that which is to come.

---

## DEATH.

Is there not an appointed time to man upon earth?

As for man, his days are as grass; as a flower of the field, so he flourisheth. For the wind passeth over it, and it is gone; and the place thereof shall know it no more.

Man that is born of a woman is of few days, and full of trouble. He cometh forth like a flower, and is cut down; he fleeth also as a shadow, and continueth not.

For what is your life? It is even as a vapor, that appeareth for a little time, and then vanisheth away.

Thou turnest man to destruction, and sayest, "Return, ye children of men." The days of our years are threescore years and ten; and if by reason of strength they be fourscore years, yet is their strength labor and sorrow; for it is soon cut off, and we fly away.

Lord, make me to know mine end, and the measure of my days, what it is; that I may know how frail I am. Behold thou hast made my days as an hand-breadth, and mine age is as nothing before thee. Surely every man walketh in a vain show. He heapeth up riches, and knoweth not who shall gather them. Thou makest his beauty to consume away like a moth. I am a stranger with thee, and a sojourner, as all my fathers were.

Help, Lord, for the godly man ceaseth; for the faithful fail from among the children of men.

Precious, in the sight of the Lord, is the death of his saints.

The Lord gave, and the Lord hath taken away; blessed be the name of the Lord.

---

## COMFORT IN SORROW.

WHEN thou art in tribulation, if thou turn to the Lord thy God, and shalt be obedient unto his voice, he will not forsake thee.

The eternal God is thy refuge, and underneath are the everlasting arms.

Weeping may endure for a night, but joy cometh in the morning.

They that sow in tears shall reap in joy. He that goeth forth and weepeth, bearing precious seed, shall doubtless come again with rejoicing, bringing his sheaves with him.

The Lord will not cast off forever; but ough he cause grief, yet will he have comassion, according to the multitude of his mercies. For he doth not afflict willingly nor grieve the children of men.

Shall we receive good at the hand of God, and shall we not receive evil?

Happy is the man whom God correcteth; for he maketh sore and bindeth up; he woundeth, and his hands make whole.

Despise not the chastening of the Lord, neither be weary of his correction; for whom the Lord loveth he correcteth, even as a father the son in whom he delighteth.

If ye endure chastening, God dealeth with you as with sons; for what son is he whom the father chasteneth not?

Though Jesus were a son, yet learned he obedience by the things which he suffered.

Now no chastening for the present seemeth to be joyous, but grievous; nevertheless afterward it yieldeth the peaceable fruit of righteousness unto them that are exercised thereby.

Blessed are they that mourn, for they shall be comforted.

For all things are for your sakes, that the abundant grace might, through the thanksgiving of many, redound to the glory of God. For which cause we faint not; but though our outward man perish, yet the inward man is renewed day by day. For our light affliction, which is but for a moment, worketh for us a far more exceeding and eternal weight of glory; while we look not at the things which are seen, but at the things which are not seen. For the things which are seen are temporal; but the things which are not seen are eternal.

For I reckon that the sufferings of this present time are not worthy to be compared with the glory that shall be revealed in us.

There remaineth therefore a rest to the people of God.

---

## IMMORTAL LIFE.

THEN shall the dust return to the earth as it was; and the spirit shall return unto God, who gave it.

God will redeem my soul from the power of the grave.

For we know that if our earthly house of this tabernacle were dissolved, we have a building of God, an house not made with hands, eternal in the heavens.

But as touching the resurrection of the dead, have ye not read that which was spoken unto you by God, saying, I am the God of Abraham, and the God of Isaac, and the God of

Jacob? God is not the God of the dead, but of the living.

For all live unto him.

It is sown in corruption, it is raised in incorruption; it is sown in dishonor, it is raised in glory; it is sown in weakness, it is raised in power; it is sown a natural body, it is raised a spiritual body. As we have borne the image of the earthy, we shall also bear the image of the heavenly.

Flesh and blood cannot inherit the kingdom of God; neither doth corruption inherit incorruption. For this corruptible must put on incorruption, and this mortal must put on immortality.

The world passeth away, and the lust thereof; but he that doeth the will of God abideth forever.

Godliness is profitable unto all things, having promise of the life that now is, and of that which is to come.

In my Father's house are many mansions; if it were not so, I would have told you.

To-day shalt thou be with me in Paradise.

Blessed are the dead which die in the Lord from henceforth. Yea, saith the Spirit; that they may rest from their labors; and their works do follow them.

They shall hunger no more, neither thirst any more; neither shall the sun light on them, nor any heat.

And God shall wipe away all tears from their eyes; and there shall be no more death, neither sorrow nor crying, neither shall there be any more pain; for the former things are passed away.

And there shall be no night there; and they need no candle, neither light of the sun; for the Lord God giveth them light.

Now we see through a glass, darkly; but then face to face. Now I know in part, but then shall I know even as also I am known.

---

## THE SPIRIT OF JESUS.

### HIS OBEDIENCE.

And the child grew, and waxed strong in spirit, filled with wisdom; and the grace of God was upon him.

He went down with his parents, and was

subject unto them, and increased in wisdom and stature, and in favor with God and man.

Though he were a Son, yet learned he obedience by the things which he suffered.

Christ suffered for us, leaving us an example that we should follow his steps; who did no sin, neither was guile found in his mouth.

He was in all points tempted like as we are, yet without sin.

## HIS OVERCOMING TEMPTATION.

And Jesus, being full of the Holy Spirit, returned from Jordan, and was led by the Spirit into the wilderness, being forty days tempted of the devil.

And the devil said unto him, "If thou be the Son of God, command this stone that it be made bread."

And Jesus answered him, saying, "It is written, 'Man shall not live by bread alone, but by every word of God.'"

And the devil, taking him up into a high mountain, showed unto him all the kingdoms of the world in a moment of time.

And the devil said unto him, "All this

power will I give thee, and the glory of them; for that is delivered unto me, and to whomsoever I will, I give it. If thou therefore wilt worship me, all shall be thine."

And Jesus answered and said unto him, "Get thee behind me, Satan, for it is written, 'Thou shalt worship the Lord thy God, and him only shalt thou serve.'"

And he brought him to Jerusalem, and set him on a pinnacle of the temple, and said unto him, "If thou be the Son of God, cast thyself down from hence; for it is written, 'He shall give his angels charge over thee, to keep thee; and in their hands they shall bear thee up, lest at any time thou dash thy foot against a stone.'"

And Jesus, answering, said unto him, "It is said, 'Thou shalt not tempt the Lord thy God.'"

And when the devil had ended all the temptation, he departed from him for a season.

And behold, angels came and ministered unto him.

And Jesus returned in the power of the Spirit into Galilee.

He was in all points tempted like as we are, yet without sin.

If any man will come after me, let him deny himself, and take up his cross, and follow me.

In the world ye shall have tribulation; but be of good cheer, I have overcome the world.

Wherefore gird up the loins of your mind; be sober; and hope to the end for the grace that is to be brought unto you at the revelation of Jesus Christ.

Thou, therefore, endure hardness, as a good soldier of Jesus Christ.

For it became him, for whom are all things, and by whom are all things, in bringing many sons unto glory, to make the captain of their salvation perfect through sufferings.

We see Jesus, who was made a little lower than the angels, for the suffering of death crowned with glory and honor.

Who, for the joy that was set before him, endured the cross, despising the shame, and is set down at the right hand of the throne of God.

### HIS FAITHFULNESS TO HIS MISSION.

The Spirit of the Lord is upon me, because he hath anointed me to preach the gospel to the poor; he hath sent me to heal the broken-hearted, to preach deliverance to the captives and recovering of sight to the blind, to set at liberty them that are bruised, to preach the acceptable year of the Lord.

I am not come to destroy, but to fulfil.

To this end was I born, and for this cause came I into the world, that I should bear witness unto the truth.

My kingdom is not of this world.

My doctrine is not mine, but his that sent me.

The Father which sent me, he gave me a commandment what I should say, and what I should speak.

And I know that his commandment is life everlasting; whatsoever I speak, therefore, even as the Father said unto me, so I speak.

My Father worketh hitherto, and I work.

Wist ye not that I must be about my Father's business?

I must work the works of him that sent me, while it is day.

I have a baptism to be baptized with, and how am I straitened till it be accomplished.

## HIS FOLLOWING GOD'S WILL.

I came down from heaven, not to do mine own will, but the will of him that sent me.

I seek not mine own will, but the will of the Father which hath sent me.

My meat is to do the will of him that sent me, and to finish his work.

Father, if thou be willing, remove this cup from me; nevertheless, not my will, but thine, be done.

And there appeared an angel unto him, from heaven, strengthening him.

And Jesus answered them, saying, "The hour is come, that the Son of man should be glorified. Now is my soul troubled; and what shall I say? 'Father, save me from this hour?' But for this cause came I unto this hour. Father, glorify thy name."

## HIS PATIENCE AND FORGIVENESS.

Bless them that curse you, and pray for them which despitefully use you. And unto him that smiteth thee on the one cheek, offer also the other.

The high-priest asked Jesus of his disciples,

and of his doctrine. Jesus answered him, "I spake openly to the world, and in secret have I said nothing. Why askest thou me? Ask them which heard me, what I have said unto them. Behold, they know what I said." And when he had thus spoken, one of the officers which stood by struck Jesus with the palm of his hand, saying, "Answerest thou the high-priest so?" Jesus answered him, "If I have spoken evil, bear witness of the evil; but if well, why smitest thou me?"

And the men that held Jesus mocked him and smote him. And when they had blindfolded him, they struck him on the face.

And when they were come to the place which is called Calvary, there they crucified him. Then said Jesus, "Father, forgive them, for they know not what they do."

When he was reviled, he reviled not again; when he suffered, he threatened not; but committed himself to him that judgeth righteously.

Put on, therefore, kindness, long-suffering, forbearing one another, and forgiving one another. Even as Christ forgave you, so also do ye.

For God sent not his Son into the world to

condemn the world, but that the world through him might be saved.

### HIS DOING GOOD TO OTHERS.

He went about doing good, for God was with him.

He hath done all things well; he maketh both the deaf to hear, and the dumb to speak.

Jesus answered and said unto them, "Go and show John again those things which ye do hear and see; the blind receive their sight, and the lame walk, the lepers are cleansed, and the deaf hear, the dead are raised up, and the poor have the gospel preached to them."

The Son of man is come to seek and to save that which is lost.

And he said unto them, "What man shall there be among you, that shall have one sheep, and if it fall into a pit on the sabbath day, will he not lay hold on it, and lift it out? How much, then, is a man better than a sheep?"

Whosoever shall give to drink unto one of these little ones a cup of cold water only, in the name of a disciple, verily I say unto you, he shall in no wise lose his reward.

The Son of man came not to be ministered unto, but to minister.

Himself took our infirmities, and bare our sicknesses.

Though he was rich, yet for your sakes he became poor, that ye, through his poverty, might be rich.

We, then, that are strong, ought to bear the infirmities of the weak, and not to please ourselves. For even Christ pleased not himself.

Bear ye one another's burdens, and so fulfil the law of Christ.

## HIS SYMPATHY WITH GOODNESS.

Whosoever shall do the will of my Father which is in heaven, the same is my brother, and sister, and mother.

Suffer little children, and forbid them not, to come unto me; for of such is the kingdom of heaven.

Whosoever shall receive one of such children in my name receiveth me; and whosoever shall receive me, receiveth not me, but him that sent me.

## HIS COMMUNION WITH GOD.

And when he had sent them away, he departed into a mountain to pray.

And he continued all night in prayer to God.

I am not alone, because the Father is with me.

I thank thee, O Father, Lord of heaven and earth, because thou hast hid these things from the wise and prudent, and hast revealed them unto babes.

Holy Father, keep through thine own name those whom thou hast given me, that they may be one, as we are. Sanctify them through thy truth. And for their sakes I sanctify myself, that they also might be sanctified through the truth. Neither pray I for these alone, but for them also which shall believe on me through their word; that they all may be one; as thou, Father, art in me, and I in thee, that they also may be one in us: that the world may believe that thou hast sent me.

O my Father, if it be possible, let this cup pass from me; nevertheless, not as I will, but as thou wilt.

Father, forgive them; for they know not what they do.

Father, into thy hands I commend my spirit.

Truly this was the Son of God.

---

## FOLLOWING AFTER THE SPIRIT OF JESUS.

THE dayspring from on high hath visited us, to give light to them that sit in darkness and in the shadow of death, to guide our feet into the way of peace.

God, who commanded the light to shine out of darkness, hath shined in our hearts, to give the light of the knowledge of the glory of God, in the face of Jesus Christ.

It is written in the prophets, And they shall be all taught of God. Every man, therefore, that hath heard and hath learned of the Father, cometh unto me.

Come unto me, all ye that labor and are heavy-laden, and I will give you rest. For my yoke is easy, and my burden is light.

I am not ashamed of the gospel of Christ;

for it is the power of God unto salvation, to every one that believeth.

The law of the Spirit of life in Christ Jesus hath made me free from the law of sin and death.

The life which I now live in the flesh, I live by the faith of the Son of God.

If any man be in Christ, he is a new creature; old things are passed away; behold all things are become new.

The love of Christ constraineth us.

We, being many, are one body in Christ.

When thou art converted, strengthen thy brethren.

Be thou an example of the believers, in word, in conversation, in charity, in spirit, in faith, in purity.

In all things showing thyself a pattern of good works.

If ye suffer for righteousness' sake, happy are ye; for Christ also hath once suffered for sins, the just for the unjust, that he might bring us to God.

Speaking the truth in love, may we grow up into him, in all things, which is the head.

Till we all come in the unity of the faith,

and of the knowledge of the Son of God, unto a perfect man, unto the measure of the stature of the fulness of Christ.

The Spirit itself beareth witness with our spirit, that we are the children of God: and if children, then heirs; heirs of God, and joint-heirs with Christ.

Beloved, now are we the sons of God, and it doth not yet appear what we shall be: but we know that, when he shall appear, we shall be like him; for we shall see him as he is.

For we all, with open face beholding as in a glass the glory of the Lord, are changed into the same image from glory to glory, even as by the Spirit of the Lord.

And every man that hath this hope in him purifieth himself, even as he is pure.

---

## PRAYER AND PRAISE.

### ASCRIPTION OF GREATNESS.

Thou, even thou, art Lord alone; thou hast made heaven, the heaven of heavens, with all their host, the earth and all things that are therein, the seas and all that is therein, and thou preservest them all; and the host of heaven worshippeth thee.

Give unto the Lord, O ye mighty, give unto the Lord glory and strength. Give unto the Lord the glory due unto his name.

Who is like unto the Lord our God, who humbleth himself to behold the things that are in heaven, and in the earth?

The Lord reigneth; he is clothed with majesty. The Lord is clothed with strength wherewith he hath girded himself. The world also is established, that it cannot be moved.

## ETERNITY OF GOD.

Lord, thou hast been our dwelling-place in all generations. Before the mountains were brought forth, or ever thou hadst formed the earth and the world, even from everlasting to everlasting, thou art God. A thousand years in thy sight are but as yesterday when it is past, and as a watch in the night.

Of old hast thou laid the foundations of the earth, and the heavens are the work of thy hands. They shall perish, but thou shalt endure. Yea, all of them shall wax old like a garment; as a vesture shalt thou change them, and they shall be changed; but thou art the same, and thy years shall have no end.

Thy kingdom is an everlasting kingdom; and thy dominion endureth throughout all generations.

## THE WONDERS OF HIS CREATION.

Bless the Lord, O my soul. O Lord, my God, thou art very great; thou art clothed with honor and majesty. Who coverest thyself with light as with a garment; who stretchest out the heavens like a curtain: who layeth the beams of his chambers in the waters; who maketh the clouds his chariot; who walketh upon the wings of the wind. Who maketh his angels spirits, his ministers a flaming fire; who laid the foundations of the earth, that it should not be removed forever.

Thou coveredst it with the deep as with a garment; the waters stood above the mountains. At thy rebuke they fled; at the voice of thy thunder they hasted away. They go up by the mountains; they go down by the valleys unto the place which thou hast founded for them. Thou hast set a bound that they may not pass over, that they turn not again to cover the earth.

In his hand are the deep places of the earth; the strength of the hills is his also. The sea is his, and he made it, and his hands formed the dry land.

Thou hast set all the borders of the earth; thou hast made summer and winter.

Thou hast prepared the light and the sun.

He appointeth the moon for seasons; the sun knoweth his going down.

The heavens declare the glory of God, and the firmament showeth his handiwork. Day unto day uttereth speech, and night unto night sheweth knowledge. There is no speech nor language where their voice is not heard. Their line is gone out through all the earth, and their words to the end of the world. In them hath he set a tabernacle for the sun, which is as a bridegroom coming out of his chamber, and rejoiceth as a strong man to run a race. His going forth is from the end of the heaven, and his circuit unto the ends of it; and there is nothing hid from the heat thereof.

The day is thine; the night also is thine.

Thou makest darkness and it is night, wherein all the beasts of the forest do creep forth. The young lions roar after their prey, and seek their meat from God. The sun ariseth; they gather themselves together, and lay them down in their dens. Man goeth forth unto his work and to his labor until the evening.

## THE SOURCE OF LIFE.

O Lord, how manifold are thy works! in wisdom hast thou made them all. The earth is full of thy riches; so is this great and wide sea, wherein are things creeping innumerable, both small and great beasts.

With thee is the fountain of life.

The eyes of all wait upon thee, and thou givest them their meat in due season. Thou openest thine hand and satisfiest the desire of every living thing.

He sendeth the springs into the valleys, which run among the hills. They give drink to every beast of the field; the wild asses quench their thirst. By them shall the fowls of the heaven have their habitation, which sing among the branches. He watereth the hills from his chambers; the earth is satisfied with the fruit of thy works. He causeth the grass to grow for the cattle, and herb for the service of man, that he may bring forth food out of the earth.

That thou givest them they gather. Thou openest thine hand; they are filled with good. Thou hidest thy face; they are troubled. Thou takest away their breath; they die and return to their dust. Thou sendest forth thy spirit; they are created, and thou renewest the face of the earth. The glory of the Lord shall endure forever. The Lord shall rejoice in his works.

## THANKS FOR HUMAN LIFE.

O, come, let us worship and bow down; let us kneel before the Lord our maker. For he is our God, and we are the people of his pasture and the sheep of his hand.

Know ye that the Lord he is God. It is he that hath made us, and not we ourselves. We are his people, and the sheep of his pasture.

He setteth the solitary in families.

Enter into his gates with thanksgiving, and into his courts with praise. Be thankful unto him, and bless his name.

O Lord, our Lord, how excellent is thy name in all the earth! who hast set thy glory above the heavens. When I consider thy heavens, the work of thy fingers, the moon and the stars, which thou hast ordained, what is man, that thou art mindful of him? And the son of man, that thou visitest him? For thou hast made him a little lower than the angels, and hast crowned him with glory and honor.

Thou madest him to have dominion over the works of thy hands; thou hast put all things under his feet; all sheep and oxen, yea, and the beasts of the field; the fowl of the air, and the fish of the sea, and whatsoever passeth through the paths of the seas. O Lord, our Lord, how excellent is thy name in all the earth!

## PROTECTING PROVIDENCE.

I remember the days of old. I meditate on all thy works. I muse on the work of thy hands.

I will open my mouth in a parable: I will

utter dark sayings of old; which we have heard and known, and our fathers have told us. We will not hide them from their children, showing to the generation to come the praises of the Lord, and his strength, and his wonderful works that he hath done. For he established a testimony in Jacob, and appointed a law in Israel, which he commanded our fathers, that they should make them known to their children; that the generation to come might know them, even the children which should be born, who should arise and declare them to their children; that they might set their hope in God, and not forget the works of God, but keep his commandments.

Our fathers trusted in thee; they trusted, and thou didst deliver them. They cried unto thee, and were delivered; they trusted in thee, and were not confounded.

We have heard with our ears, O God, our fathers have told us, what work thou didst in their days, in the times of old.

One generation shall praise thy works to another, and shall declare thy mighty acts.

I will lift up mine eyes unto the hills, from whence cometh my help. My help cometh from the Lord, who made heaven and earth. He will not suffer thy foot to be moved. He that keepeth thee will not slumber. Behold he that keepeth Israel shall neither slumber nor sleep. The Lord is thy keeper; the Lord is thy shade upon thy right hand. The sun shall not smite thee by day, nor the moon by night. The Lord shall preserve thee from all evil; he shall preserve thy soul. The Lord shall preserve thy going out and thy coming in, from this time forth and even forevermore.

Except the Lord build the house, they labor in vain that build it; except the Lord keep the city, the watchman waketh but in vain. He giveth his beloved sleep.

## THANKS FOR DELIVERANCE.

O, give thanks unto the Lord, for he is good; for his mercy endureth forever. Let the redeemed of the Lord say so, whom he hath redeemed from the hand of the enemy, and gathered them out of the lands, from the east, and from the west, from the north, and from the south. They wandered in the wilderness in a solitary way; they found no city to dwell in. Hungry and thirsty, their soul fainted in them. Then they cried unto the Lord in their trouble, and he delivered them out of their distresses. And he led them forth by the right way, that they might go to a city of habitation. O that men would praise the Lord for his goodness, and for his wonderful works to the children of men! For he satisfieth the longing soul, and filleth the hungry soul with goodness.

They that go down to the sea in ships, that do business in great waters, — these see the works of the Lord, and his wonders in the deep. For he commandeth and raiseth the stormy wind, which lifteth up the waves thereof. They mount up to the heaven, they go down again to the depths; their soul is melted because of trouble. They reel to and fro, and stagger like a drunken man, and are at their wits' end. Then they cry unto the Lord in their trouble, and he bringeth them out of their distresses. He maketh the storm a calm, so that the waves thereof are still. Then are they glad because they be quiet; so he bringeth them unto their desired haven.

O that men would praise the Lord for his

goodness, and for his wonderful works to the children of men!

He turneth the wilderness into a standing water, and dry ground into water-springs. And there he maketh the hungry to dwell, that they may prepare a city for habitation, and sow the fields and plant vineyards, which may yield fruits of increase. He blesseth them also, so that they are multiplied greatly, and suffereth not their cattle to decrease. He setteth the poor on high from affliction, and maketh him families like a flock.

I waited patiently for the Lord, and he inclined unto me and heard my cry. He brought me up also out of an horrible pit, out of the miry clay, and set my feet upon a rock, and established my goings. And he hath put a new song in my mouth, even praise unto our God.

Many, O Lord my God, are thy wonderful works, which thou hast done, and thy thoughts which are to us-ward. They cannot be reckoned up in order unto thee; if I would declare and speak of them, they are more than can be numbered.

O magnify the Lord with me, and let us

exalt his name together. I sought the Lord, and he heard me, and delivered me from all my fears. This poor man cried, and the Lord heard him, and saved him out of all his troubles.

The Lord was my stay; he brought me forth also into a large place.

In the day when I cried, thou answeredst me, and strengthenedst me with strength in my soul.

I love the Lord, because he hath heard my voice and my supplications. Because he hath inclined his ear unto me, therefore will I call upon him as long as I live. The sorrows of death compassed me, and the pains of hell got hold upon me; I found trouble and sorrow. Then called I upon the name of the Lord: "O Lord, I beseech thee, deliver my soul." Gracious is the Lord, and righteous; yea, our God is merciful. The Lord preserveth the simple; I was brought low, and he helped me. Return unto thy rest, O my soul, for the Lord hath dealt bountifully with thee. For thou hast delivered my soul from death, mine eyes from tears, and my feet from falling. I will walk before the Lord in the land of the living.

What shall I render unto the Lord for all his benefits toward me? I will pay my vows unto the Lord now, in the presence of all his people.

### THANKS FOR GUIDANCE.

I will bless the Lord, who hath given me counsel. I have set the Lord always before me; because he is at my right hand, I shall not be moved.

My mouth shall praise thee with joyful lips, when I remember thee upon my bed, and meditate on thee in the night-watches. Because thou hast been my help, therefore in the shadow of thy wings will I rejoice. My soul followeth hard after thee; thy right hand upholdeth me.

I have remembered thy name, O Lord, in the night, and have kept thy law. I thought on my ways, and turned my feet unto thy testimonies. At midnight I will rise to give thanks unto thee, because of thy righteous judgments. Before I was afflicted, I went astray, but now have I kept thy word. It is good for me that I have been afflicted, that I might learn thy statutes. Unless thy law had been my delight, I should then have perished in mine affliction. I will never forget thy precepts, for with them thou hast quickened me. I have seen an end of all perfection; thy commandment is exceeding broad. O how I love thy law! It is my meditation all the day.

I am continually with thee; thou hast holden me by my right hand. Thou shalt guide me with thy counsel, and afterward receive me to glory.

### DESIRING COMFORT IN SORROW.

My God, my God, why hast thou forsaken me? I cry in the day-time, but thou hearest not; and in the night season, and am not silent.

O that I knew where I might find him! that I might come even to his seat. I would order my cause before him, and fill my mouth with arguments.

Hear my cry, O God; attend unto my prayer. From the end of the earth will I cry unto thee, when my heart is overwhelmed; lead me to the rock that is higher than I.

Be merciful unto me, O God, be merciful unto me; for my soul trusteth in thee. Yea, in the shadow of thy wings will I make my refuge, until these calamities be overpast.

Will the Lord cast off forever; and will he be favorable no more? Hath God forgotten to be gracious? hath he in anger shut up his tender mercies?

My tears have been my meat, day and night, while they continually say unto me, "Where is thy God?" When I remember these things, I pour out my soul in me. Why art thou cast down, O my soul? and why art thou disquieted in me? Hope thou in God; for I shall yet praise him for the help of his countenance.

O my God, my soul is cast down within me. Deep calleth unto deep, at the noise of thy water-spouts; all thy waves and thy billows are gone over me. Yet the Lord will command his loving-kindness in the day-time, and in the night his song shall be with me, and my prayer unto the God of my life.

Why art thou cast down, O my soul? and why art thou disquieted within me? Hope thou in God; for I shall yet praise him who is the health of my countenance and my God.

## FAITH AND CONFIDENCE.

The Lord is my light and my salvation; whom shall I fear? The Lord is the strength of my life; of whom shall I be afraid?

Though a host should encamp against me, my heart shall not fear; though war should rise against me, in this will I be confident.

One thing have I desired of the Lord, that will I seek after, — that I may dwell in the house of the Lord all the days of my life; to behold the beauty of the Lord and to inquire in his temple.

For in the time of trouble he shall hide me in his pavilion; in the secret of his tabernacle shall he hide me; he shall set me up upon a rock.

I had fainted, unless I had believed to see the goodness of the Lord, in the land of the living. Wait on the Lord; be of good courage, and he shall strengthen thy heart. Wait, I say, on the Lord.

God is our refuge and strength, a very present help in trouble. Therefore will not we fear, though the earth be removed, and though the mountains be carried into the midst of the sea;

though the waters thereof roar and be troubled, though the mountains shake with the swelling thereof.

The Lord God is a sun and shield; the Lord will give grace and glory; no good thing will he withhold from them that walk uprightly. O Lord of hosts, blessed is the man that trusteth in thee.

My soul, wait thou only upon God; for my expectation is from him. He only is my rock and my salvation; he is my defence; I shall not be moved. In God is my salvation and my glory; the rock of my strength and my refuge is in God. Trust in him at all times, ye people. Pour out your heart before him; God is a refuge for us.

## FOR FORGIVENESS.

Out of the depths have I cried unto thee, O Lord.

Have mercy upon me, O God, according to thy loving-kindness; according unto the multitude of thy tender mercies, blot out my transgressions. Wash me thoroughly from mine iniquity, and cleanse me from my sin; for I acknowledge my transgressions, and my sin is ever before me. Against thee, thee only, have I sinned, and done this evil in thy sight.

For thy name's sake, O Lord, pardon mine iniquity, for it is great.

If thou, Lord, shouldest mark iniquities, O Lord, who shall stand? But there is forgiveness with thee, that thou mayest be feared.

Remember, O Lord, thy tender mercies and thy loving-kindnesses, for they have been ever of old. Remember not the sins of my youth, nor my transgressions; according to thy mercy remember thou me, for thy goodness' sake, O Lord.

Hide thy face from my sins, and blot out all mine iniquities. Create in me a clean heart, O God, and renew a right spirit within me. Cast me not away from thy presence; and take not thy holy spirit from me. Restore unto me the joy of thy salvation, and uphold me with thy free spirit. O Lord, open thou my lips, and my mouth shall show forth thy praise. For thou desirest not sacrifice, else would I give it. The sacrifices of God are a broken spirit; a broken and a contrite heart, O God, thou wilt not despise.

I wait for the Lord; my soul doth wait, and in his word do I hope. My soul waiteth for the Lord more than they that watch for the morning; I say, more than they that watch for the morning.

## THE MERCY OF GOD.

Bless the Lord, O my soul, and all that is within me bless his holy name. Bless the Lord, O my soul, and forget not all his benefits; who forgiveth all thine iniquities, who healeth all thy diseases; who redeemeth thy life from destruction; who crowneth thee with loving-kindness and tender mercies.

He hath not dealt with us after our sins, nor rewarded us according to our iniquities. For as the heaven is high above the earth, so great is his mercy toward them that fear him. As far as the east is from the west, so far hath he removed our transgressions from us. Like as a father pitieth his children, so the Lord pitieth them that fear him. For he knoweth our frame; he remembereth that we are dust.

As for man, his days are as grass; as a flower of the field, so he flourisheth; for the wind passeth over it, and it is gone, and the place thereof shall know it no more. But the mercy of the Lord is from everlasting to everlasting upon them that fear him, and his righteousness unto children's children, to such as keep his covenant, and to those that remember his commandments to do them.

Bless the Lord, ye his angels, that excel in strength, that do his commandments, hearkening unto the voice of his word. Bless ye the Lord, all ye his hosts; ye ministers of his that do his pleasure. Bless the Lord, all his works, in all places of his dominion. Bless the Lord, O my soul.

## TRUST.

The Lord is my shepherd; I shall not want. He maketh me to lie down in green pastures; he leadeth me beside the still waters. He restoreth my soul; he leadeth me in the paths of righteousness for his name's sake. Yea, though I walk through the valley of the shadow of death, I will fear no evil: for thou art with me; thy rod and thy staff they comfort me.

Thou preparest a table before me in the

presence of mine enemies: thou anointest my head with oil; my cup runneth over.

Surely goodness and mercy shall follow me all the days of my life, and I will dwell in the house of the Lord forever.

### GOD'S BLESSING ON THE RIGHTEOUS.

The earth is the Lord's, and the fulness thereof; the world, and they that dwell therein; for he hath founded it upon the seas, and established it upon the floods. Who shall ascend into the hill of the Lord? or who shall stand in his holy place? He that hath clean hands and a pure heart; who hath not lifted up his soul unto vanity, nor sworn deceitfully. He shall receive the blessing from the Lord, and righteousness from the God of his salvation.

### THE SECURITY OF THE RIGHTEOUS.

He that dwelleth in the secret place of the Most High shall abide under the shadow of the Almighty. I will say of the Lord, "He is my refuge and my fortress, my God, in him will I trust."

Surely he shall deliver thee from the snare of the fowler and from the noisome pestilence. He shall cover thee with his feathers, and under his wings shalt thou trust. His truth shall be thy shield and buckler.

Thou shalt not be afraid for the terror by night, nor for the arrow that flieth by day, nor for the pestilence that walketh in darkness, nor for the destruction that wasteth at noonday. A thousand shall fall at thy side, and ten thousand at thy right hand; but it shall not come nigh thee. Only with thine eyes shalt thou behold and see the reward of the wicked.

Because thou hast made the Lord, which is my refuge, even the Most High, thy habitation, there shall no evil befall thee, neither shall any plague come nigh thy dwelling. For he shall give his angels charge over thee to keep thee in all thy ways. They shall bear thee up in their hands, lest thou dash thy foot against a stone. Thou shalt tread upon the lion and adder; the young lion and the dragon shalt thou trample under feet.

Because he hath set his love upon me, therefore will I deliver him; I will set him on high because he hath known my name. He shall call upon me, and I will answer him. I will be with him in trouble; I will deliver him and honor him. With long life will I satisfy him, and show him my salvation.

## PRAYER FOR WISDOM.

Unto thee, O Lord, do I lift up my soul. Show me thy ways, O Lord; teach me thy paths. Lead me in thy truth, and teach me; for thou art the God of my salvation: on thee do I wait all the day.

O that my ways were directed to keep thy statutes. Then shall I not be ashamed, when I have respect to all thy commandments. Wherewithal shall a young man cleanse his way? By taking heed thereto according to thy word.

Open thou mine eyes, that I may behold wondrous things out of thy law. Make me to go in the path of thy commandments, for therein do I delight. So shall I keep thy law continually; and I will walk at liberty.

Thy word is a lamp unto my feet, and a light unto my path. The entrance of thy words giveth light; it giveth understanding unto the simple.

Order my steps in thy word, and let not any iniquity have dominion over me. Quicken me, O Lord, according to thy loving-kindness.

Cause me to know the way wherein I should walk. Teach me to do thy will, for thou art my God. Thy Spirit is good; lead me into the land of uprightness. Quicken me, O Lord, for thy name's sake.

## SENSE OF GOD'S PRESENCE.

O Lord, thou hast searched me and known me. Thou knowest my down-sitting and mine up-rising; thou understandest my thought afar off. Thou compassest my path and my lying-down, and art acquainted with all my ways. For there is not a word in my tongue, but lo, O Lord, thou knowest it altogether. Thou hast beset me behind and before, and laid thy hand upon me. Such knowledge is too wonderful for me; it is high; I cannot attain unto it. Whither shall I go from thy Spirit? or whither shall I flee from thy presence? If I ascend up into heaven, thou art there. If I make my bed in the grave, behold thou art there. If I take the wings of the morning and dwell in the uttermost parts of the sea, even there shall thy hand lead me, and thy right hand shall hold me. If I say, Surely the darkness shall cover me, even the night shall be light about me. Yea, the darkness hideth not from thee; but the night shineth as the day. The darkness and the light are both alike to thee.

Search me, O God, and know my heart; try me, and know my thoughts. And see if there be any wicked way in me, and lead me in the way everlasting.

## DEVOUT LOVE.

O God, thou art my God, early will I seek thee. My soul thirsteth for thee, my flesh longeth for thee in a dry and thirsty land, where no water is. Because thy loving-kindness is better than life, my lips shall praise thee. Thus will I bless thee while I live; I will lift up my hands in thy name. My mouth shall praise thee with joyful lips, when I remember thee upon my bed, and meditate on thee in the night-watches.

As the hart panteth after the water brooks, so panteth my soul after thee, O God. My soul thirsteth for God, for the living God.

How precious are thy thoughts unto me, O God! how great is the sum of them! If I should count them, they are more in number than the sand. When I awake, I am still with thee.

Whom have I in heaven but thee? and there is none upon earth that I desire besides thee. My flesh and my heart fail, but God is the strength of my heart and my portion forever.

One thing have I desired of the Lord, that will I seek after; that I may dwell in the house of the Lord all the days of my life, to behold the beauty of the Lord, and to inquire in his temple.

## MORNING DEVOTION.

My voice shalt thou hear in the morning, O Lord; in the morning will I direct my prayer unto thee, and will look up.

I laid me down and slept; I awaked; for the Lord sustained me.

O God, thou art my God; early will I seek thee; my soul thirsteth for thee. My mouth shall praise thee with joyful lips, when I remember thee upon my bed, and meditate on thee in the night-watches.

My heart is fixed, O God, my heart is fixed; I will sing and give praise. Awake, psaltery and harp! I myself will awake early. I will praise thee, O Lord, among the people.

The mighty God, even the Lord, hath spoken, and called the earth, from the rising of the sun unto the going down thereof. Out of Zion, the perfection of beauty, God hath shined.

Lord, lift thou up the light of thy countenance upon us.

O, send out thy light and thy truth; let them lead me; let them bring me unto thy holy hill, and to thy tabernacles.

## PRAISE FOR DAILY BENEFITS.

Blessed be the Lord, who daily loadeth us with benefits.

The lines are fallen unto me in pleasant places; yea, I have a goodly heritage.

I will praise thee, O Lord, with my whole heart; I will show forth all thy marvellous works. I will be glad and rejoice in thee. I will sing praise to thy name, O thou Most High.

Thou wilt shew me the path of life. In thy presence is fulness of joy. At thy right hand there are pleasures forevermore.

I will bless the Lord at all times; his praise shall continually be in my mouth.

O, magnify the Lord with me, and let us exalt his name together.

While I live will I praise the Lord; I will sing praises unto my God while I have any being.

I will extol thee, my God, O king, and I will bless thy name for ever and ever. Every day will I bless thee, and I will praise thy name for ever and ever.

## THANKS FOR RAIN.

Praise waiteth for thee, O God, in Zion, who art the confidence of all the ends of the earth, and of them that are afar off upon the sea.

Who by his strength setteth fast the mountains, being girded with power; who stilleth the noise of the seas, the noise of their waves, and the tumult of the people. They also that dwell in the uttermost parts are afraid at thy tokens; thou makest the outgoings of the morning and evening to rejoice.

Thou visitest the earth, and waterest it; thou greatly enrichest it with the river of God, which is full of water. Thou preparest them corn, when thou hast so provided for it. Thou waterest the ridges thereof abundantly. Thou settlest the furrows thereof. Thou makest it soft with showers. Thou blessest the springing thereof. Thou crownest the year with thy goodness, and thy paths drop fatness.

They drop upon the pastures of the wilderness, and the little hills rejoice on every side. The pastures are clothed with flocks. The valleys also are covered over with corn. They shout for joy; they also sing.

## IN STORM AND TEMPEST.

The Lord reigneth ; let the people tremble. He sitteth between the cherubim ; let the earth be moved.

The floods have lifted up, O Lord, the floods have lifted up their voice; the floods lift up their waves. The Lord on high is mightier than the noise of many waters, yea, than the mighty waves of the sea.

The voice of the Lord is upon the waters; the God of glory thundereth; the Lord is upon many waters.

His lightnings enlightened the world; the earth saw and trembled.

The voice of the Lord is powerful; the voice of the Lord is full of majesty. The voice of the Lord breaketh the cedars; yea, the Lord breaketh the cedars of Lebanon. The voice of the Lord divideth the flames of fire. The voice of the Lord shaketh the wilderness. The Lord sitteth upon the flood; yea, the Lord sitteth king for ever.

God is our refuge and strength, a very present help in trouble. Therefore will we not fear though the earth be removed, and though the mountains be carried into the midst of the sea; though the waters thereof roar and be troubled; though the mountains shake with the swelling thereof.

The Lord will give strength unto his people; the Lord will bless his people with peace.

The Lord reigneth; let the earth rejoice. Clouds and darkness are round about him; righteousness and judgment are the habitation of his throne.

## THANKFUL PRAISE.

O, give thanks unto the Lord, for he is good; for his mercy endureth forever.

O, give thanks unto the God of gods; O, give thanks to the Lord of lords.

To him who alone doeth great wonders;

To him that by wisdom made the heavens;

To him that stretched out the earth above the waters;

To him that made great lights;

The sun to rule by day,

The moon and stars to rule by night;

To him that led his people through the wilderness;

Who remembered us in our low estate;

Who giveth food to all flesh; for his mercy endureth forever.

O, give thanks unto the God of heaven; for his mercy endureth forever.

## JOYFUL WORSHIP.

O, sing unto the Lord a new song; sing unto the Lord, all the earth. Sing unto the Lord, bless his name; show forth his salvation from day to day.

O, worship the Lord in the beauty of holiness; fear before him, all the earth.

Say among the heathen that the Lord reigneth, the world also shall be established, that it shall not be moved. He shall judge the people righteously.

Let the heavens rejoice, and let the earth be glad; let the sea roar, and the fulness thereof.

Let the field be joyful, and all that is therein; then shall all the trees of the wood rejoice before the Lord.

For he cometh, for he cometh to judge the earth. He shall judge the world with righteousness, and the people with his truth.

## PRAISE FROM ALL PEOPLE.

The Lord is in his holy temple; let all the earth keep silence before him.

Praise waiteth for thee, O God, in Zion; and unto thee shall the vow be performed. O thou that hearest prayer, unto thee shall all flesh come.

God be merciful unto us and bless us, and cause his face to shine upon us. That thy way may be known upon earth, thy saving health among all nations. Let the people praise thee, O God; let all the people praise thee. O, let the nations be glad, and sing for joy; for thou shalt judge the people righteously, and govern the nations upon earth. Let the people praise thee, O God; let all the people praise thee. Then shall the earth yield her increase, and God, even our own God, shall bless us. God shall bless us, and all the ends of the earth shall fear him.

## PRAISE FROM ALL NATURE.

Praise ye the Lord. Praise ye the Lord from the heavens. Praise him in the heights. Praise ye him, all his angels. Praise ye him, all his hosts. Praise ye him, sun and moon; praise him, all ye stars of light. Praise him, ye heaven of heavens, and ye waters that be above the heavens.

Let them praise the name of the Lord; for he commanded, and they were created. He hath also established them for ever and ever. He hath made a decree which shall not pass.

Praise the Lord from the earth, ye dragons and all deeps; fire and hail; snow and vapor; stormy wind fulfilling his word; mountains and all hills; fruitful trees and all cedars; beasts and all cattle; creeping things and flying fowl; kings of the earth and all people; princes and all judges of the earth; both young men and maidens, old men and children; let them praise the name of the Lord: for his name alone is excellent; his glory is above the earth and heaven.

Praise ye the Lord.

## PRAISE WITH MUSIC.

Praise ye the Lord. Praise God in his sanctuary. Praise him in the firmament of his power.

Praise him for his mighty acts; praise him according to his excellent greatness.

Praise the Lord with harp; sing unto him with the psaltery and an instrument of ten strings; sing unto him a new song; play skilfully with a loud noise. For the word of the Lord is right, and all his works are done in truth.

Praise him with the sound of the trumpet; praise him with the psaltery and harp.

Praise him with the timbrel and dance; praise him with stringed instruments and organs.

Praise him upon the loud cymbals; praise him upon the high-sounding cymbals.

Let everything that hath breath praise the Lord.

Praise ye the Lord.

## GLORY IN THE HIGHEST.

Glory to God in the highest; and on earth peace, good-will to men.

Thou art worthy, O Lord, to receive glory and honor and power; for thou hast created all things.

Hallelujah! Salvation and glory and honor and power unto the Lord our God.

Praise our God, all ye his servants, and ye that fear him, both small and great.

Hallelujah! for the Lord God omnipotent reigneth!

---

## BENEDICTION.

The Lord bless thee and keep thee; the Lord make his face shine upon thee, and be gracious unto thee; the Lord lift up his countenance upon thee, and give thee peace.

The Lord our God be with us, as he was with our fathers; let him not leave us, nor forsake us.

The Lord will give strength unto his people; the Lord will bless his people with peace.

Now the God of peace, that brought again from the dead our Lord Jesus, that great Shepherd of the sheep, make you perfect in every good work to do his will, working in you that which is well-pleasing in his sight.

And the peace of God, which passeth all understanding, keep your hearts and minds through Christ Jesus.

# INDEX.

GOD.—*His Existence.*



*His Spiritual, Eternal Nature.*



*His Presence.*



*His Power.—In Nature.*



*His Power.—Among Men.*

PATIENCE.



CHARITY AND FORGIVENESS.



DOING GOOD TO OTHERS.



LOVE.



HUMAN BROTHERHOOD.



SPIRITUAL LIFE.

DEATH.



COMFORT IN SORROW.



IMMORTAL LIFE.



THE SPIRIT OF JESUS. — *His Obedience.*



*His Overcoming Temptation.*



*His Faithfulness to his Mission.*



*His Following God's Will.*



*His Patience and Forgiveness.*

*Thanks for Deliverance.*



*Thanks for Guidance.*



*Desiring Comfort in Sorrow.*



*Faith and Confidence.*



*For Forgiveness.*



*The Mercy of God.*



*Trust.*



*God's Blessing on the Righteous.*



*The Security of the Righteous.*



*Prayer for Wisdom.*



*Sense of God's Presence.*



*Devout Love.*



*Morning Devotion.*



*Praise for Daily Benefits.*

THE END.

MAY 22 1917

Cambridge: Electrotyped and Printed by Welch, Bigelow, & Co.

www.ingramcontent.com/pod-product-compliance
Lightning Source LLC
LaVergne TN
LVHW021406110826
845150LV00007B/1812